Fire
MY CPA

An Entrepreneur's Guide to Financial Success and Massive Tax Savings

SARAH JONES

LUCIDBOOKS

Fire My CPA:
An Entrepreneur's Guide to Financial Success and Massive Tax Savings
Copyright © 2024 by Sarah Jones, CPA

Published by Lucid Books in Houston, TX
www.LucidBooks.com

ISBN: 978-1-63296-694-0
eISBN: 978-1-63296-695-7

Special Sales: Most Lucid Books titles are available in special quantity discounts. Custom imprinting or excerpting can also be done to fit special needs. Contact Lucid Books at Info@LucidBooks.com

To Pappy Joel.

My father, the one who is my hero and taught me what hard work was.
If I grow up to be even a tenth of what your character and heart is,
I will consider that a successful life lived.

Table of Contents

What is Fire My CPA?

Before I get way into the meat and the potatoes of this book and what we're going to offer—and before I have a CPA reaching out with hate mail—let's answer a few questions.

First, why is this book titled *Fire My CPA?*

I'm not saying that you should fire your Certified Public Accountant and do your own accounting. Instead, Fire My CPA is a play on marketing from a nerdy CPA. Chances are, when you saw the title of this book, it was a gut punch. You felt the pain of, *"Oh my gosh, I totally relate to that."* But this book is not in any way, shape, or form your DIY accounting guide. That would be a path to destruction, being audited, lack of clarity, and fear. Hear me say this: You need a CPA. You just need a good CPA.

Something we say here at Sarah Jones CPA all the time is: *Taxes suck. Make sure your CPA doesn't.*

If your CPA does not give you clarity, or if you do not feel empowered by that relationship, it's a problem. If they're not an entrepreneur, not cutting-edge and staying on top of all the new tax legislation, they're driving a 1985 Toyota Corolla, have a pocket protector, and do everything by paper, I can guarantee that person is not like-minded with an entrepreneur who wants to grow their business.

You need a licensed CPA who is a hardcore nerd and loves what they do, but that is also like-minded and can follow a conversation with you, from A to B and all the way to Z for every goal you want to achieve.

Fire My CPA is from a CPA who's seen a lot of different things in our industry. We're looking at what you need in a CPA, what you absolutely don't need in a CPA, and how to know if your CPA is good or bad. We'll also consider why it's absolutely necessary that you work with a CPA and the steps to say, "What's the cost of actually continuing this relationship with a bad CPA?"

I'll help you discover what a good CPA should do, what you should look for, and give you the tools that you need to make an educated decision to answer the questions, "Is my CPA enough for me? Do I need to look elsewhere?"

Then we'll look at interviewing other CPAs. We'll ask, "Who's the best fit for me?" When you get a CPA who is like-minded, and they're on the same page with you, it's a huge game changer. Partnering with a quality CPA gives you a solid return on your investment that can take you far—no matter where you're starting.

A good CPA will give you clarity. A good CPA will take away fear. A good CPA will give you education. A good CPA should be able to take something complex and simplify it in a way that anyone can understand. A good CPA will be honest and will communicate with you. A good CPA will even be honest with you if they make a mistake. They'll fess up, and they'll make it right.

CPAs are not perfect, but again, this book isn't here to advocate for a DIY approach. I do not recommend that at all, given the extreme consequences that could result.

So, why does an entrepreneur or businessperson need a CPA? Look at the subtitle of this book. You need a CPA to reach financial success (based on your goals) and to maximize tax savings.

Before I was a CPA, I only had my EA (Enrolled Agent) license. Many people don't even know what that is, but basically it means that you're licensed federally by the IRS in all 50 states. An EA is typically somebody that specializes in messy tax situations.

I wanted to make sure that I had the ability to represent taxpayers, so I started with my EA license. An EA is typically a very good credential, but if you're a business owner, you're better off working with a CPA. If you ever have to go through a due diligence process, or if you are going to sell your company, you will need a CPA for the audit. Anytime you need an audit, or any type of assurance, review, or attestation, you have to use a CPA. So, if the person you're currently working with is not a CPA, you may end up paying more to have a second person come in and do the job. Working with a licensed CPA is just like going to a medical doctor—it ensures that they have gone through a board that is governed by the state.

Every state is different, but it's a strenuous amount of work to even qualify to be a CPA, so it makes sure the person you're working with is held to a higher standard. They know what they're doing.

I'm a CPA in the state of Texas, so when I finished my master's degree in accounting, I first had to go and get a certain amount of hours in training. Even though I had a master's degree, I had to apply to be accepted to even sit for the CPA exam. Once accepted, I had to go through those rigorous exams. It was hard work, but it was worth it. After passing the four exams, I had to go through a background check. And then, and only then, could I *apply* as a CPA.

Our industry has a very dark side to it. A lot of people just assume that their tax preparer is a CPA. You always need to ask. But it's also important to realize that no one has to be licensed to do tax or to do bookkeeping, and in some states, you can even call yourself an accountant without being a CPA. Let's say Bob wanted to call himself a tax preparer. Bob could go to the IRS website today and get a free number called a PTIN number. This is what tax preparers are given. He could start preparing tax returns tomorrow with absolutely no experience.

In the state of Texas, you cannot say that you're an accountant or do accounting work without being a licensed CPA. I'm passionate about these standards, but even here there are issues I see.

I was in a mastermind very early in my career. I became associated with a group who said they did bookkeeping. It was very surprising, and scary, that they were also giving poor advice and consulting clients on tax matters, although they had absolutely no experience whatsoever.

My point is, you want to make sure that you are working with a qualified CPA. If you're not sure about the person you've hired, you first need to ask if they are a CPA and, if they're not, you need to find a CPA. *Fire My CPA* is all about how to make sure your CPA is a good one, because there are a lot of bad ones out there. One of the biggest things that I find on TikTok and Instagram is people in the tax profession who are not licensed. They are not CPAs, and they always say, *"Man, your CPA is just a number cruncher. They don't do any strategy, blah, blah, blah."*

I agree. I'm fully on board with the criticism against lack of strategy (more on that later), but that is not to say that you should go get with a tax strategist. That is not a CPA. You need both. You need a CPA who also provides these services. It is kind of like going to see a doctor who says, "I can do the latest, greatest things, but you know what? I'm actually not a Medical Doctor." You do not want to put your financial health, your financial stability, or your financial future at risk. You need to work with the CPA.

If you're currently working with someone, your number one checklist item is to ask them what their credentials are and get proof of it. I will tell you, if you have somebody who just helps you with tax on that tax return, at the very bottom, it will have their PTIN number. It'll say what firm they're with. If they're a CPA, most of the time, CPA will be behind their name. If not, that does not necessarily mean that they're not a CPA. You need to ask.

Again, the point of *Fire My CPA* is not to suggest you start DIY accounting that will get you somewhere you do not want to go. We're saying, you need to ask, "Is my CPA doing a good job?" Most likely, if you picked this book up, your gut's already answering you.

What is a good CPA? What makes a CPA bad? How can I make sure the person I align myself with for my business and personal life, for both short-term and long-term goals, will be a good match for me so I don't have to keep searching for a CPA?

That's what *Fire My CPA* is for. It's to answer those questions so you can experience both financial success and massive tax savings.

Let's get started.

Who is Sarah Jones CPA?

Who is Sarah Jones, CPA? Whenever I start reading a new book, I always want the author to tell me why I should read this book. Who are they, and why are they an authority on this subject?

I don't read fiction books. I'm one of those nerdy people who only read self-improvement, health books, how to increase profits by X—you get the idea. I love it. I'm a sucker for it. So, I always go to the author section because I want to know, is this just a marketing ploy, or do they know what they're talking about? Because of the fact that the name of my book is *Fire My CPA*, and because of the fact that I am a CPA, I want to give you some background on who I am, and why I'm qualified to talk about this subject. I understand that some of my clients will probably read this book, but I know a larger population of the people that will read this book are not clients.

Most readers don't know Sarah Jones, CPA. So, why listen to me? I'm not here to toot my own horn, but I'll give you a bit of background. You can't hear my twang, but I'm a country girl from Willis, Texas, raised by a very good family, and I'm passionate about accounting. I'm a Certified Public Accountant in the state of Texas. I'm also an Enrolled Agent and licensed by the IRS in all 50 states on a federal level to represent taxpayers in all 50 states. Beyond that, I'm a Certified Tax Planner and a Certified CFO.

Educationally, I have my undergraduate degree in Business Administration. I got my Master of Business Administration and Finance, and I have a Master of Science Degree in Finance. I also have a Master of Science and Accountancy degree. So yes, I have three master's degrees. I also have a Certificate in Financial Management from Cornell University.

As you can tell, I highly, highly value education. It's something that was instilled in me when I was young. Again, I'm not tooting my own horn. I just know my stuff, and I want you to understand that the things that I'm telling you come from over 15 years of experience in the industry, plus many certifications and degrees. I'm writing this book because I am truly passionate about educating people and making sure they have the tools they need to succeed.

As for my upbringing, I was raised in Willis, Texas, about an hour north of Houston. I'm the youngest of three kids. My father was in construction. He worked—a lot. My father was the hardest working person I've ever met. He worked two or three jobs at a time, and we never saw him because he worked so much. He knows how to work hard, and he inherently feels like everybody is lazy. I often feel the same way. I got that from him.

My mom was able to stay home with us because my dad worked so hard, but when we got a little bit older, she became a housekeeper and cleaned houses to make extra money. I got married at a very young age, and I was able to live in Hawaii for two years and then in Virginia for two years. After going through an awful divorce, I became a single mom practically overnight— which is not something that I wanted or even expected.

Through that experience, I came back to Texas with no money in my bank account. I ended up living with family until I could get on my feet.

And you know what? It kind of pissed me off.

I wasn't through school yet. I was still working on my bachelor's degree. When my daughter (who is now in college) was three and I was 24, I put myself through graduate school. I would work all day, then come home, and spend time with her, and then she would go to bed. I would make a pot of coffee, and I would go to work. I poured myself into working. For years, I worked my way up to a budget analyst, then a management role, and other positions in between.

My last role was as a senior accountant for a very large municipality here in Texas. It was at a great organization with mostly great leadership, but my immediate boss was awful and was not a good leader or communicator. She was very volatile in her personality and quite vindictive. One day she came in and blamed me for something that had happened—a project that I wasn't even involved with. She took it out on me, and she even threw papers at me. That was the last straw. I went home and told my husband, Phil, "I kind of want to go out on my own."

I'll never forget what he said to me. "Sarah, worst case scenario, let's say that you try this, and you suck, and you're awful at it. You just go get another job. You have three master's degrees and 15 years of experience. You are going to be able to get a job."

His worst-case-scenario advice really resonated with me. It gave me the confidence I needed because I had a lot of fear in stepping out there, and fear is a big factor when it comes to our finances; something we will talk a lot about throughout this book.

When I first started my business, I probably made every single mistake in the book. I almost got into business relationships with organizations and CPAs who were not actually certified. So, I learned to ask important questions of the CPAs I interviewed. There were CPAs who wanted to offer their services, but they were not qualified, and did not do good work. They didn't have their best interest or their clients' best interests at heart. And through that, I created Sarah Jones CPA, because I had seen such a bad side of the industry, and I didn't want that for my clients. I'm very passionate about making sure clients get educated, get the tools they need to be successful, and that everyone understands they need a CPA. Those letters, C. P. A., are so important.

So, to answer the question, *Who is Sarah Jones?* I assure you that I do know what I'm talking about. Most importantly, I am highly qualified and credentialed, with your best interest at heart. I am passionate about giving you the information, education, and tools that you need to be able to make good decisions. Your financial life spills over and transposes into so many other areas of your life.

Money is not everything, but it's up there. Money is not evil, nor is money good; money is neutral. It's what you do with it that matters. Money is a tool to get you from here to where you want to go. You need a CPA who will also view it as such and will journey with you. And that means that you might have to fire your current CPA.

CHAPTER 1

Identifying the Gap

I often hear the same complaints about someone's CPA. They never hear from them. When they do hear from them, they have no idea what they're talking about. Because of this, they feel like they don't know if their financial situation can get better—they don't know what they don't know. They have no idea what a CPA should or should not do. They stay with their CPA because at least that is safe. They're full of fear, they have no answers, they don't have clarity, but they stay with their CPA. So, why might your current CPA not be enough? Ask yourself this question: do you feel empowered by your taxes and your financials?

If you don't get reports, that is a huge red flag. But let's say you get those reports on a monthly basis, and if you are not empowered or don't have the tools and education necessary to be able to look at those reports and understand them—that means that you haven't had the necessary meetings with your CPA to read those. That's a telltale sign that your CPA may not be enough. Another issue is when they send your tax return to you on an annual basis. If it looks like gibberish, you need to reach out to your CPA to actually get clarity to go through that. But if you have a CPA who does not go through your tax return with you, that is another huge red flag that your CPA may not be enough.

A lot of people don't understand that when you sign that tax return, you are liable for it. Even though you go to a CPA to do that tax return for you, you are the taxpayer in the eyes of the IRS. You should fully understand and go through that tax return. You are fully liable for everything on those forms. If you email your CPA and two weeks go by and you have to send them another email because they have not responded, that's not saying that your CPA is a bad CPA, but it means that your CPA is not a good business owner.

Another telltale sign that your CPA may not be enough, especially for business owners and entrepreneurs, is a wide age gap. Nothing against our elders, but if your CPA is 70 years old with a pocket protector, if they drive a 1985 Chevrolet or a Toyota Corolla, and if they do everything on paper, they have not stayed up with the times.

You want a CPA who hustles, is motivated, and has heart and goals like yours. If they don't, they're not going to align with you on a values basis or the things that are important to your business.

Yes, you need a CPA. But you need a good CPA. You need a CPA who's going to understand your mindset and your goals. When your CPA is not enough, you're left with fear, which holds you back. When you are held back and when you are paralyzed with fear, you cannot achieve your goals.

Financial goals transpose and spill over into all facets of your life. I'm a numbers girl to the core. I truly feel that health and wealth go hand-in-hand. They're the two things whose value we don't understand until we don't have them. You need to protect and nurture these throughout your life, through habits, and through daily practices. A good CPA will want you to be wealthy. They will want you to have a healthy mindset. They will want you to succeed. They will encourage you in your goals.

And you know what? A good CPA will also call you out on your crap. A good CPA will tell you, "Hey, you've told me that this has been your goal and you're really not being accountable."

You need a CPA who's very clear on how they operate and what they do—and those expectations should be set from the beginning.

What are some important things to expect? You should not be able to get the CPA on the phone the first time you call them—if they don't have an assistant, it's a red flag. You should not be able to immediately get in to see them. If you are going to your doctor, you fully expect that you're going to go through their system. You'll talk to their administrative office manager, and they're going to set you on that doctor's schedule because that means that doctor is good. He's educated, he's credentialed, and he's in high demand. You want a CPA who has a proven track record of success, who is in demand, but who can accommodate you. That's the key.

Here's your checklist to know if your CPA isn't sufficient:

- Your gut told you to pick up this book.
- They do not communicate well or break complex tasks down in what I call Flintstone style.
- They do not have systems and processes in place for when you contact them.
- You continue to find errors in the things that they do.

For example, let's say that you tell your CPA, "I've sold my house this year. What do you need from me?" And he says, "Great. Congratulations. I'm going to need all of your documents. I'm going to need a list of all your improvements, and then I also need your closing statements showing what you sold it for and the date it sold." You send it all to your CPA on February 15th. On April 14th, the CPA comes back to you and says, "Hey, here's your return," and the house isn't even in the return. That is a key indicator that your CPA may not be enough for you. That example shows a CPA who is overworked and doesn't have processes in place to accommodate his clients and their needs.

I want to help you through this journey and identify if your current CPA is enough, and what to do if they aren't. Do we extend an olive branch and give them another chance? If not, I want to give you the tools that you need to know what kind of CPA can accommodate both your short-term and your long-term needs. It's time to close the gap.

CHAPTER 2

Not to Hate on CPAs

I want to put a disclaimer out here right now. I am a CPA, and I'm not coming after CPAs. CPAs are the highest, most educated form of accountant. I say that loosely because different states have different regulations. You need to make sure you work with a CPA, but I am going to call out some CPAs, purely because I am one. I have been in this industry of accounting and bookkeeping and tax, and I've done this for over 15 years, in many different facets of the industry. I know what a good CPA is, and I absolutely know what a bad CPA is. This book is not meant to hate on CPAs. This is about what you need as a client and holding CPAs accountable. I would guess that a lot of people that pick up this book are going to be business owners and entrepreneurs.

You need people like a doctor, an attorney, or a financial advisor in your life at different times, and you need to make sure that there's synergy between you, that you're like-minded. Your CPA should be a trusted fiduciary. You're going through your journey with them. They need to be on the same page with you, and you want to make sure that you stick with them.

Sometimes it happens. Sometimes you get with a CPA or a different professional and things don't work out, or you just don't feel like it's a good fit, so you go in search of another professional. What I don't want you to do is hop from CPA to CPA trying to find this. I want to give you the tools that you can use to say, *Okay, I'm going to go interview five CPAs and I'll know exactly what I'm looking for.*

I'm actually going to give you a tangible checklist that you can use in your search for a new CPA. So again, no hate mail from CPAs. I am one. You need a CPA. You just need to make sure it's a good one.

With that in mind, we'll look at what you need and how to know your CPA doesn't suck.

First, your CPA must have a CPA designation.

We're going to go through this in more detail, but I have clients all the time who follow accountants online. This involves limitations. Online state statutes have different requirements. A lot of people inherently just assume that their tax preparer or their bookkeeper is a CPA, but it's up to you to confirm that. I know a lot of great professionals that do great work, and they love their clients, and they are not a CPA, but what ensures that you have success—and mitigates your risks—is making sure they have credentials.

You need to ensure that the person you're working with is like-minded, that they're a hustler, an entrepreneur, that they can understand your goals, and answer questions. They should be able to take a complex issue, hold a conversation, break it down in a way that you can actually understand it, and make you feel empowered by it to help guide your decision-making process.

By far, the biggest complaint that I've heard from new clients about their past experience is, "I called my CPA but couldn't get him on the phone. They said to send an email, so I emailed, but that was last Thursday. I emailed again this week, and before I know it, it's been literally four weeks before I'm getting a response."

Maybe your CPA is not a bad CPA, but they clearly don't have systems and processes set up. They're not a great business owner, and they do not have time for you. You need a CPA who has the team, the systems, and the processes in place so that no matter how big they grow, their business is scalable, and they can still actually take care of their clients and nurture those relationships. They should give you the service you need despite their growth. That's the CPA you need.

CHAPTER 3

The High Cost of Financial Complacency

I often find it's easier to look at a situation by comparing it to something similar. So, let's consider how wealth can be illustrated by health. For example, you're supposed to be eating well, you joined a gym, and you have a great trainer, but you know what? It's really stressful, and it's a lot easier to stay at home. So, you've been eating at home and just going out now and then.

But they opened up a great new Mexican restaurant in your town. Let's say that you're eating a few too many cheese enchiladas and you're having a little bit too much wine. You're not counting your calories, you're not getting your workouts in, and most importantly, you're not getting on the scale every Friday and checking in with your trainer.

You should be okay, right?

No.

That right there is being complacent. It's that spot where you're comfortable. It feels good. It's easy, but it's the most dangerous place to be because no change occurs. It further integrates and drives those bad habits, but it especially takes you further away from your goals. Not only do you fail to achieve your goals, but you're probably going to gain unwanted weight. You're going to be more tired and less likely to do the stuff that you're supposed to do. That's complacency.

Okay, so let's put that into financial terms. Let's say that you are with a CPA, and they do a good job. They have those credentials behind their name and gave you everything you need, so you know that they know what they're doing. But let's say that you don't hear from them all year.

You follow up with them a couple of times, and you don't get called back. In September, you're trying to reach out, and you're having a hard time. You've emailed a couple times, and you can't get in for an appointment. You're feeling that nervousness in your gut and figure, *we'll just do this next year.*

That's financial complacency. I've had over 15 years of experience, seeing all different sides of the industry, including the dark side of accounting, while also seeing the really good side of the industry. Ultimately, it led to starting my own firm based on all of my knowledge to give clients what they need and want. But it's up to you to hold your CPA to those standards.

I want to go through a few different scenarios, because our firm at Sarah Jones CPA offers many services. We do accounting and bookkeeping. We do CFO services, we do taxes, and we do tax planning. We're about to integrate full-service wealth management. But whatever services you need, there are so many ways you may find yourself demonstrating complacency.

Who pays for the cost of financial complacency? It's not your CPA—it's you. The taxpayer/business owner pays for it.

Bookkeeping

So, let's look at bookkeeping. I've seen this many times with clients that come to us. They reach out to us for bookkeeping. They say, "Sarah Jones CPA, we need help because we signed up for bookkeeping services with the CPA company, and we're supposed to be getting monthly reports, and it's been six months, and I haven't gotten my reports."

That's the cost of financial complacency. In that situation, you're supposed to have monthly reports, and a quarterly review meeting. But you realize it's been six months, and you haven't had any reports at all. You have no idea of what's going on. You don't even know if your books are being reconciled. They're sure as heck charging you, but you're not seeing any work. Then you're also not having your check-in meeting.

So, let's say this goes on for six months. It's November, and you finally get ahold of them and they're like, "Oh my gosh, I'm so sorry. We've had lots of staff change and blah, blah, blah. Karen is your new account manager, and she will get you set up for a meeting." You get a meeting for December.

A very small percentage of companies might be on a fiscal year, but let's assume that your year end is December 31st. So, you go to your meeting, and you haven't seen anything for six months. You're meeting with somebody completely new because of the company's turnover. Of course, Karen's super nice, but Karen doesn't know anything about your business because she's brand new on your account. She sees that in the last six months nothing has even been reconciled. You're supposed to have a meeting to see where you're going financially. But Karen tells you, "I'm really excited to be working on your account, but I have six months of catchup I have to do; so let's schedule another meeting on December 22nd, okay? "

She needs time to get all this stuff up to date. So, you have to go through all of these questions that you've already told your last person, but Karen doesn't have notes on that. Karen finally gets your stuff updated. At last, you think you're back on a good path. Then you have your follow-up meeting at the end of December with Karen, and she sends you your reports, and again, you haven't been reconciled and the bookkeeping hasn't been done.

This is with a company that you've paid money to do this for the last six months, and she finally gives it to you. You see that your net income is double what it was last year. You're a business owner and you're smart, so you knew that things were going well, but you didn't know your income was that high.

You go through it all with Karen and she says, "Yeah, we got it updated. Here are your financials for the last six months. Just for example, last year your net income was $400,000. This year so far, you're on track for $800,000 of net income."

Well, because the company didn't do your bookkeeping for six months and because you didn't have six months of reports and because no follow-up was done, you had no idea that your tax liability went way through the roof. You didn't update your estimated tax payments, and you had an opportunity last month to invest in a new project, and your cash flow is gone. You wanted to take advantage of that opportunity because you didn't have the clarity, the education, or the empowerment of a team that would do your bookkeeping.

I see that literally every single week because we have those people calling our team at Sarah Jones CPA. That is what we specialize in—keeping everything together.

Chief Financial Officer

The second example I want to give you is with a Chief Financial Officer. Maybe you need more than bookkeeping. Let's say that you are making over a million dollars a year. You have a lot of stuff going on, and you have big goals. That's what CFO coaching is for. I have clients all the time that were signed up for fractional CFO coaching or fractional CFO services, and they come to me, and I heard the same scenario as the bookkeeping client.

"We signed up. We were promised the world, here's our contract. We're paying $3,000 a month for this. I haven't heard from anyone in six weeks. I can't get anyone on the phone. We're supposed to get a weekly update. I haven't gotten any of my monthly reports. I go into QuickBooks. None of my stuff's updated."

What CFO clients need is clarity on their cash flow and to know what they can and can't do. CFO services are very custom. You basically come to Sarah Jones CPA and say, "Look, my goal is A, B, and C." We create a roadmap for success on how you get those dreams to actually come to fruition, and then we keep you accountable. We call you out on your crap when needed, and we keep you on track to actually achieve those goals. We see CFOs drop that all the time. Like with the bookkeeping client, CFOs don't know how profitable they've been, and they're not prepared for their tax bill. A CFO client may not be sure if they can take an opportunity. Usually, a CFO service tracks cash flow and cash flow drivers. Without that input, they have no idea what they can do.

Let's say there was a massive opportunity that they should have absolutely taken advantage of, and they didn't because they didn't have the real time information to make those decisions in their business. That is the high cost of financial complacency, as well as bookkeeping and CFO services.

Tax

But now, let's talk about tax. I could talk about tax forever. I hear the exact same things all the time. "I don't know what I'm paying. I have no idea how I'm taxed. Do I need to be paying this year? Do I have an estimate? What do I do if my income goes up?" By far, the cost of financial complacency and tax is working with the CPA who is not proactive. At Sarah Jones CPA, you get a weekly newsletter, because you need to know what's going on with your money.

You get a monthly video with me bugging you about deadlines, updates, and anything relevant. You get a monthly invitation to book on my calendar for a consult. What I tell every single client is that at the bare minimum, I want to talk to you. I want to see you face-to-face four times a year because you do not know if you can or cannot do something. I cannot advise you properly if we're not communicating.

By far, the highest cost of financial complacency in tax is when you have a taxpayer who does their taxes in April or they have their CPA file an extension, but they're not getting business done until September and October. Finally, all they do is send you the return. *Here's your bill. Pay the IRS this amount.*

Otherwise, you're not hearing from them at all. It's like crickets until the next filing season, and then you get there, and they file an extension, and the cycle continues. That is the most inefficient, unproductive, and the costliest way that you can manage your tax relationship with the CPA. Your CPA should be bugging you. Even if it's too much for you, you want that compared to someone who you never hear from.

Again, at Sarah Jones CPA, you get a monthly newsletter on every single new piece of legislation, as well as tax reminders. I do custom videos based on everything that's going on for that month that is blasted to all of our tax clients, to all of our bookkeeping clients, all of our tax planning clients, and all of our CFO clients.

Why? This relationship is important, and the cost of financial complacency is high. When new clients come over, they say, "I need a CPA because I can't get a hold of my CPA. I've tried to get meetings all year. This happened last year. I told her I needed more communication. I called, but I never got a call back. I emailed. I never was able to get in. I need more communication."

They come over to me, but it's already past September because they've tried and they've tried, and they've extended that olive branch, and that CPA didn't give them what they need. We go in, and we get their books clean, and we see what's going on. Their income is way higher than they thought, and they've used cash flow on capital purchases and improvements, and they don't have money available to pay their tax bill, they're freaking out—simply because they weren't proactive in transitioning sooner. They trusted their CPA was doing their job, despite the lack of communication.

If you're coming to your CPA in January, most of those things have to be done by December 31st, which means you have to do them before December 31st, and get with your CPA and figure out what makes sense. That is an extremely high cost of financial complacency that I see time and time again. At least once a week, we get a new client because they are not satisfied with their CPA and because it's too late. We do what we can, but a lot of times we can't fix it because they are in arrears. You can't go back and do things on the prior year for tax planning.

At Sarah Jones CPA, we offer a completely free tax analysis. That means we have a secure portal where you can go and upload your prior tax returns, both business and personal. I go in personally and do all the tax analysis myself.

I look at how you're set up and I can quickly tell, "Oh, man, this isn't good, or, Hey, this is great." I've been offering free analysis for tax since 2018. I have never once had a client who's been absolutely good, and for whom I don't find a single issue. For that, the highest cost of financial complacency is not getting tax planning. Maybe your CPA actually does communicate well, plus they're credentialed, they're licensed, and things are going pretty well, but you just kind of always felt like you were overpaying.

You didn't really quite understand why you were being taxed the way you are, and you kind of wanted to ask, but you didn't want to seem like you're stupid, and you felt like you should know—but you don't. You don't ask because you don't want things (the relationship) to become uncomfortable. That's a dangerous place of complacency.

I've had clients come over to me and give me their tax return. I stare at them, and literally look around for Ashton Kutcher because I must be getting *Punk'd.* That's how bad some of these tax returns are. They're technically clean and accurate returns, but that's not enough.

They're usually from a CPA who did the tax return without educating their client that there's a different way to get more bang for your tax buck. A lot of times with a client like that, I will go to them, and I'll say, "Hey, I actually looked at your return, and I could have saved you $27,000 last year." I literally had one like this yesterday, and inherently it's always the same. They always get really mad at their CPA and I say, "Wait, hold on. I see that this is CPA X." A lot of times, if it's a local client, I know the CPA, and I know that technically they're a well-educated and good CPA. They're not the kind of CPA who you want though. It doesn't mean they're a bad CPA, just not the CPA you want.

I'll say, "Your CPA did your return right, and it's clean. But they didn't do tax planning. Did you ask them to do tax planning?" Usually, the client will tell me they didn't, and I address that it's not completely on their CPA.

Before you fire your CPA, we'll have checklists of what you should and shouldn't look for.

Tax Planning

One of the highest costs of financial complacency is found in the lack of tax planning. I have so many clients who are paying self-employment tax on their earnings.

One, they don't even know what self-employment tax is because they don't have a CPA who educates them. Two, they have no idea they can completely and legally avoid self-employment tax because their CPA is not educating them. There is a different way to actually do this. Outside of that, I get larger clients who have multiple companies, and they're really inefficient in the way that the income flows. It's good to have a CPA who will work with a really good attorney group to do some restructuring and make their taxation efficient and strategic.

On average, very conservatively speaking, Sarah Jones CPA saves our clients and business owners an average of 20% to 30% on their taxes each and every year with proper planning. Those clients are signing up, and we have a tax planning engagement. I do that free analysis and create them a custom-built tax planning package. A lot of times it will involve some restructuring with a qualified attorney. Then, they're proactive, and we meet on a quarterly basis, making sure everything's in line. We'll meet, and they'll tell me anything new that's come up so I can accommodate and make sure we're being strategic. With this procedure, tax time is a breeze. We already have everything cleaned up, because most of the time, we're doing their bookkeeping and their CFO work.

We have monthly reports sent to them. We have check-ins every quarter to go over tax. Then, at tax season, we already know everything. There's already been an estimate. It's the most strategic and efficient tax that we can get, and then we're just reconciling and reporting everything at the end of the year, and it's not this scary unknown.

The cost of financial complacency is an absolute lack of clarity, lack of education, and lack of knowledge—and it costs you huge. It's missed opportunities on capital-boosting projects that you could have done if you had known where you were. It's the overpaying of tax that I see every single week with new clients coming to Sarah Jones CPA because they don't have a CPA who will go down that road with them.

Financial complacency is extremely dangerous. Again, it's kind of like that diet you were supposed to be on, that workout you were supposed to be doing, and instead you're eating chips and queso and not getting on the scale. You need a CPA who will give you the tools you need, give you an exact roadmap for success, and will nudge your arm a little bit to keep you on track and make sure you get from point A to point B.

CHAPTER 4

Hidden Risks of a Mismatched CPA

What does it mean to potentially be mismatched with your CPA? We've gone through what *Fire My CPA* is all about and why you actually need to make sure you're working with a CPA, as well as some of the downfalls and darker sides of our industry. But how do you know that you could be mismatched?

We're going to look at some indicators and a summary before we jump into this one. If you're reading this book, it's probably a good indication that you're mismatched because the term *Fire My CPA* probably hit you in the gut. I would assume that if somebody was very happy and pleased with their CPA, and they saw this book, it's not something they would pick up, because it doesn't appeal to them.

So, the first indicator you may be mismatched with your CPA is that you're reading this book. Second, there is an indicator if your CPA isn't communicating. Like we said before, if you send emails, and it's taking weeks to get a response, or you have to keep following up, that's definitely a sign of a mismatch with your CPA. The third issue is if your CPA doesn't match your values. For example, if you're a business owner or an entrepreneur, like most of our clients here at Sarah Jones CPA, you want a CPA who is in line with that thinking. They should have goals that can help navigate better than a paper-pushing CPA.

Another sign is that you have to ask for tax planning and extra explanations of your finances. When you ask why your tax bill is the way that it is, it's a problem if your CPA simply says, "Well, that's just the way it is."

It's okay to give them the benefit of the doubt. There are some instances, for example, if you're a W2 earner, you cannot go to the IRS and say that you just want to partake in tax planning and not have federal income tax withheld. It's a very small percentage, but you could be in that bracket. But if you ask your CPA questions and they're just saying, "That's the way that it is," instead of giving you an explanation and clarification—that is a flag that you're definitely mismatched with your CPA.

Another sign that you're mismatched with your CPA is if your CPA does not offer all-encompassing services. If you're a business owner, you need bookkeeping services, CFO services, accounting, tax services, tax planning, insurance services, wealth services, and possibly even a legal team.

Your CPA needs to do all of those things or have access to them. For example, I am a CPA, and we have a CPA firm, and we're all encompassing. I'm not a licensed attorney, but we work very closely with an attorney group whom we share clients with. We work as a team together for the benefit and the value-add in the strategy of our clients.

Find a CPA like that. Find someone who looks at you holistically and knows there is a synergy with getting as much service as you can in one place. So, if you have a CPA who only does tax, that is an important sign that you're mismatched.

Where does a mismatched relationship lead?

CHAPTER 5

Uncovering Inefficiencies and Missed Opportunities from a Mismatched CPA

A mismatched CPA isn't necessarily a bad CPA, it's just a CPA who isn't a match for your financial needs and goals. And when you work with a CPA who is a mismatch, you will experience inefficiencies and missed opportunities, both of which can be killers of a growing business. So what are the inefficiencies and missed opportunities that happen by working with a CPA who is a mismatch? We're going to go through a lot of them because there are many negative patterns. Again, I've been in this industry for over 15 years. I've seen a lot of the good, and I've seen a lot of the bad.

One of the first inefficiencies is when your tax return is done by a paper pusher, a data entry person. Some tax returns are super straightforward. If you're a W2 employee, and you have one W2, that's an easy return, and perfect for the companies that specialize in easy returns. But most of the people who work with a CPA are

23

not just a simple W2. Most of the time they're business owners and entrepreneurs who have a lot going on.

They need a CPA who's not just a paper pusher.

By default, most CPAs who are involved in tax start their business, put up shop, and they literally just do taxes for any person who comes to them. They do that work because they need the income, and it becomes a stack of papers on a desk of a few thousand returns. They do the bare minimum work to be compliant, just to get that paper across their desk so that they can bill and be done for the year. They don't start out to be paper pushers, but that's what they become.

If you want a paper pusher, go to a local tax prep company, like the ones you see set up in Walmart during tax season. Those people have no proper education—they just go through a six-week tax course. That is not what you're wanting as a business owner who values your money.

I have my master's degree in accounting, but even after investing those hours and getting the knowledge that I needed for that CPA exam, I was not taught tax strategy in any way, shape, or form. I was taught how to keep a client compliant. I was taught IRS rules. I was taught the guidelines. I was taught the Generally Accepted Accounting Principles (GAAP). These are all extremely important and show why it's important to go with a CPA who has a good education. But as a CPA, we are not taught how to do tax strategy. We're not taught how to run a business. We're not taught customer service. Those are things we must be driven to learn on our own so we can be more than just paper pushers. A great CPA is passionate to be the total package for their clients.

The second inefficiency we've mentioned is when your CPA does no tax planning. They're just doing the returns.

I'll be honest—with every single return I look at, I look for opportunity. A lot of times, by the time I get the return, it's too late. If a new client comes to me, and it's already past December 31st, there's nothing I can do for the year that I'm actually preparing. I do, however, always go through to see if there's opportunity going forward.

In my years as a CPA, I've had maybe one or two clients say, "I don't want to talk to you about strategy. I literally just want you to do my tax return." I absolutely respect that, if that's what they want and need. But the majority of my clients are excited and say, "This is what I've been searching for, for years! I need someone who can give me the information, the tax strategy, and the tools that I need."

If your CPA doesn't do planning, I can guarantee you're overpaying at least by 20% to 30%. If you're a business owner without a tax strategy, you're not taking advantage of every tax advantage you're entitled to.

The next inefficiency is high turnover. If your CPA office assigns you a new preparer every year, that's a red flag. They may not inherently be a bad CPA, but is this the person who's best aligned with you and what you want both in the short-term and the long-term? If there is high turnover, that most likely means it's not an organized, healthy organization, and there's probably a reason why they have high turnover.

It's a problem if you're constantly being given someone new and every year you're having to say, "My name is Bob, and y'all have done my tax return for 10 years, but let me explain to you, again . . ."

That's frustrating to handle year after year. It probably also gives you a little bit of fear. Worst of all, it's almost like you're getting a new tax preparer, and that creates a potential for inefficiency. The chance of an error goes way up when turnover is high.

The biggest inefficiency that I see with a mismatched CPA is you overpay on your taxes if you're with a CPA who isn't proactive, doesn't keep up with the trends, and doesn't stay at the forefront of any tax legislation. If they're not passionate about tax planning and saving you money, you are overpaying your hard-earned dollars to the IRS.

You do have to pay tax. I get that, but I don't like the tax. Nobody likes tax. I would rather find a way to legally use the IRS code and do planning that will decrease the amount I give to the IRS. I'm a much better steward of my money than the IRS is, and you can be too. At Sarah Jones CPA, we have a tax system. For every single person who comes to Sarah Jones CPA, whether a brand-new client or somebody that we work with every single year, we look for money-saving opportunities.

Most good CPAs do all-encompassing, cumulative work. They do bookkeeping, they do CFO, they do tax, they do tax planning, they focus on being a one-stop shop. There's a lot of synergy created there. When you have a mismatch with a CPA who offers some, but not all of those, you're missing out.

Let's say that you are with a CPA, and they do your bookkeeping and your tax work, but they're not doing a great job on the bookkeeping work. How do you know that?

If you have your bookkeeping done monthly by a CPA, and you're not getting reports every single month, that is a red flag for inefficiency. It's kind of like being on a diet and not getting on the scale for feedback.

Another indication is when you have no clarity on your cash flow. Maybe you're getting your reports, but you don't understand them, and you never get any feedback or opportunities to meet and go through them.

Another huge red flag is when you don't understand the financial reports they give you. If you're with a CPA and they're giving you the report monthly, but you don't understand it, there's a problem. If you do not have a clear understanding of your financials, your profit and loss, your balance sheet, your statement of cash flows, or any of your KPI dashboards, you need a meeting. Every CPA is a little different, but at Sarah Jones CPA, depending on the needs, some of our clients want a once-a-month meeting. Some of them don't want meetings built into their monthly package, and they have the option to request a meeting and book on our calendar a la carte.

Let's go back to our personal trainer example. If you go to a trainer, you want a certified trainer. You're going to make sure you work with somebody certified. You wouldn't just go get Joe Blow off the street because he said he knows how to work out. You're going to go with somebody certified.

You go to him, he makes you a great plan, with great workouts, but maybe he gives you a specific exercises and you're like, "I don't know what any of this is." Perhaps the plan says lateral raises and back squats and stiff leg deadlifts, for example. If you do not go to that trainer and get clarity on what those exercises are, you're not going to be able to integrate and put them directly into your life to actually get the results that you need.

Likewise, if you're working with a CPA, and they're giving you reports, but you have no idea of what any of it means, you need to ask them. A good CPA will set up a meeting to educate you on the topic. Education is empowerment. When there's empowerment, there is success for the client.

A lack of clarity is an inefficiency, especially if it keeps you from making decisions on the fly in your business. If you're not getting reports, and you're stuck in a place where you cannot make a decision because you don't have the data on the other side, you need clarity.

But maybe the CPA *is* giving you the data. However, if you don't feel empowered by those numbers or you don't understand them, it's like getting the plan from a trainer and not knowing what the exercises are. You're not going to be able to use that data to make a decision that you need to on the fly. You need a CPA who will educate you on your financials so you can integrate and use the data to make decisions for your business.

On the topic of clarity, if you're running your business without a goal, what are you doing? If you're running your business without an exit plan, what are you doing? God gave us this one life and we're blessed to have it. If you are not working every single day towards something, you need a CPA who will help you.

What's another red flag that you have a mismatched CPA? You can't take advantage of opportunities because you have no understanding of where you are financially. This is very interrelated with the last few points that we've talked about, but I've had this come up many times as a consequence of those issues. I've had clients literally come to us and say, "Okay, Sarah, I've been trying to get with my CPA for six months. I have this opportunity in real estate. I cannot get my financials. My banker needs this. I need help and I need help fast."

It's so unfortunate, because without good communication, the client didn't know there was an issue. He assumed everything was up to date. But when he had an opportunity arise, his CPA wasn't prepared. and the client paid the price.

Having a solid CPA in place who will give you everything you need and keep you clean and compliant every single month will make all the difference. It means you can take advantage of any opportunity that arises.

The last big sign that you're working with a mismatched CPA is that you have no long-term goals or vision. Your CPA should sit with you at some point and say, "Hey, let's talk. What's your plan here? Do you have an exit plan? Are you putting money aside? Are you making sure that you're investing for your future? Let's talk about your kids. Do you have enough insurance? Do you have your will?"

I'm not a licensed attorney, but I am in it for the long haul for my clients. I want to make sure that my clients have everything they need to succeed. I'm not going to draft a will, but I have a really good attorney I work with literally on a weekly to monthly basis for my clients.

You want your CPA to do that. If you're going through this chapter and thinking, *I didn't even know a CPA could do this or should do this*, I'm here to tell you that you need to go search for a good CPA who has your best interest at heart. You want to interview a CPA and see if they match your goals. And then, you work with them, and you'll find an incredible amount of synergy and strategy and peace, and it really takes away all of the fear that can creep into your financial life when you have a mismatched CPA.

CHAPTER 6

Lack of Communication and Resulting Fears

As we've discussed in previous chapters, a lack of communication is a huge issue, but the resulting fear from that lack of communication is even worse.

When people come to Sarah Jones CPA, we always ask how they found out about us, but I also ask, "Why are you looking for a new CPA?" Some of the new clients are new business owners, and they don't have a CPA. Most of them, however, are current business owners who have worked with another CPA. The issue is often the same. "I never hear from my CPA and, when I do, I have no idea what they're talking about."

Communication is the key. If you look at successful militaries throughout history, communication is vital. If you want to win a battle, get rid of communication on the opposing side. Communication is key in marriage, family, and any type of relationship. And it's at the forefront of what you need from your CPA as well.

Clients of Sarah Jones CPA get a weekly email with tax tips, breaking news, and anything relevant. They get a video from me once a month, saying, "Hey, how's it going? Do we need to do a consult? Remember, these specific deadlines are coming up. This is this time of year you have blah, blah, blah, blah, blah."

That's what you need from your CPA. Without that communication, you experience all of those inefficiencies that we talked about. You end up with a paper pusher, and there's no planning. You have high turnover, and you have no clarity on your cash flow, or you don't understand your financials.

You can't make decisions in your business that way. You can't take advantage of opportunities without an adequate understanding and planning with your CPA. You'll have no accurate long-term goals or vision because you don't know where you are today. From a financial standpoint, you'll absolutely overpay in taxes, and that can amass to hundreds of thousands of dollars over your lifetime.

But ultimately, it results in uncertainty. It creates a mindset of fear, and nobody wants to operate out of fear. When you operate out of fear, you're not being authentic. You're not bringing forth your best self.

Decisions made based in fear are not the best decisions. I could probably write a separate book about fear, because I feel like we've all been through that, but I will tell you a quick story.

When I first started my business back in 2015, I quickly realized the impact of fear. We make decisions out of fear for a few reasons. One, we face financial pressures. We may not have our systems set up, and we don't have confidence yet. So, thinking of a new business owner who doesn't have a great CPA, they hand over all their stuff at year end and the CPA may not ask necessary questions and takes months to do it.

After following up repeatedly, the business owner gets this tax bill and feels so confused. By the time the tax bill arrives, it's already next year, and they haven't even planned.

That process will lead you to operate in fear. You need a CPA who removes that fear from you. I'll be honest, I've had conversations with clients where I've said, "You know what? I really feel like you're operating out of fear right now. I want you to take a deep breath. I want you to settle down, and let's make this a more productive call, okay?"

Unexpected things do happen, especially if you're a business owner. Let's say that expenses are up, and profits are down. You can get emotional, but that is operating out of fear and is not the best way to make decisions. You need a CPA to help you operate out of peace and adequate understanding, to look at things in an unbiased, clear way so you can navigate those different seasons of your business. Operating out of fear leads to making bad decisions.

You're going to be guided by false assumptions, and you're going to have a lack of empowerment. Again, your finances and your relationship with your CPA should give you a breath of fresh air. It should give you clarity. A good CPA wants to make you the CEO of your life. We like to give you clarity in your financials. We like to give you excellent work that you can count on, and we like to give you out of the box thinking, because most people in your circle will be thinking in your box.

Find a CPA who has your best interest at heart and is going to help you to operate outside of fear.

CHAPTER 7

Long-Term Consequences of a Mismatched CPA

When it comes to mismatched CPA relationships, inefficiencies and missed opportunities, a lack of communication, and the resulting fears from that, what does it all mean? Generally, there are long-term consequences of staying with the wrong CPA. It isn't just a little here and there.

At first, the relationship's kind of frustrating, but they're saving you money.

No, it's more than that if you picked up this book. If you were completely satisfied with your CPA, you would not have picked up this book. That's the best indicator that you may need to look for another CPA.

There's no communication and, ultimately, you are overpaying on your taxes, even if you don't realize it. That's really what it comes down to. The ultimate clincher that should hit you in the gut is that by using a poorly matched CPA, you are going to overpay on your taxes by hundreds of thousands of dollars—potentially millions, depending on how much business you have over your lifetime.

Do you want to potentially overpay by hundreds of thousands, or even millions, of dollars in unnecessary tax to the IRS that, with the proper CPA, could be money in your pocket? Maybe your CPA is a great CPA, but he's not a great CPA *for you*. He may be a good CPA for somebody that has a W2 and needs simple work.

Remember we talked about those CPAs who do paper pushing? You don't want a paper pusher. It's going to cost you. If you don't have the clarity and don't know exactly what's going on in your business, if you don't have a pulse on your cash flow, if you don't have long-term and short-term goals, if you don't have a CPA who will call you out on those goals if necessary, and if they're not being proactive, and if you're not communicating with them, it is costing you significant dollars in tax over your lifetime. We can't sugarcoat the reality. It's your tax dollars. Yes, you need everything.

You need a CPA who will save you money and go to bat for you. You need a CPA who will be strategic and will be on your side. You want someone who will be there long-term for you, to help you right now and as your business grows—and even as you exit your business at some point in your life. Just like a trusted advisor, I'm required to be a fiduciary for my clients. That means I'm required to do what's best for them. That's what you need. I can't say it any other way.

We're going to say it one more time—a mismatched CPA, with inefficiencies, a lack of communication, and a fear mindset means that you overpay by hundreds of thousands of dollars to potentially millions of dollars over your lifetime in unnecessary tax.

Is that a long-term consequence you're willing to carry?

I want to give you a few examples of the true cost and how this can play out in your life through some true stories that come from people I've worked with at Sarah Jones CPA. As a CPA, I cannot disclose my clients, so the names and minor details have been changed, but the story is the same and they're all true.

So, let's talk about Lorena. Lorena is a client that came to me for tax season at the beginning of February. She had been with her CPA for many years, and there was such comfort in staying with that CPA, but she wasn't satisfied. She understood there was a mismatch. There was no communication, on top of many of the other issues we've looked at.

She came to me in February. She had a trucking company, and her CPA was supposed to be doing her bookkeeping. She hadn't been getting her monthly report, so she tried reaching out, emailing, and calling. Lorena was out there hustling and bustling, trying to make a buck, trying to grow her business, and it kind of got put on the back burner as it does for a lot of my clients. I completely understand that as an entrepreneur.

She was going to potentially take advantage of getting some new vehicles, and she needed it for her growth, but she didn't know if it was in the budget. She didn't know if she could afford it or if there were tax benefits there. Again, she had reached out to her CPA, five or six different times, but could never get with them.

After the CPA went MIA, Lorena came to me in February of 2021. Well, in the tax year 2021, any equipment purchases over 6,000 pounds, which hers were, could be depreciated, or she could take the bonus depreciation of a hundred percent. Lorena had quite a large taxable income, but she was not able to get the clarity to make that move. She way overpaid in tax. Had she invested in those trucks like she wanted to, it would have completely wiped out her tax bill. She would have those new assets that would have given her room to almost double her business over the next couple of years.

It really was unfortunate, because one of the stipulations of taking advantage of that bonus depreciation is the asset has to be placed in service by December 31st. In our case, she would have had to have purchased the vehicles and had ownership of them in hand on her lot by December 31st, which she could have done if she was able to communicate with her CPA. Lorena missed a chance that would have wiped out her tax bill and doubled her business in a couple of years.

That is a true, hit you in your gut, mismatched CPA with tons of inefficiencies. And what was the end result? She massively overpaid in her tax and, through that process and without clarity and the contact and communication, she was operating out of fear.

But Lorena isn't alone. Rolando was a real estate investor, who came to me in March because he, too, had a CPA who was completely MIA. Rolando could not get him on the phone. As a real estate investor, Rolando wanted to purchase a property. The bank wanted his last year's tax return, which he had, so he was able to give that over. But they had some questions on his real estate properties, his transactions, and they wanted a profit and loss on each property. It looked like his prior CPA hadn't reflected those accurately on his tax returns.

So, he needed that information. But none of his efforts to reach his CPA made a difference. There was an opportunity Rolando really wanted to take advantage of, but couldn't because he didn't have the accurate records. He didn't have his financials. There was no clarity. He had no idea what he was looking at.

The opportunity passed him by, a property that would have given him great cash flow and would have been a great addition to his portfolio. He had to let that go. It got sold out from underneath him because he did not have what he needed for his banker. Why? Because his CPA could not provide it to him.

Let's talk about Sally. Sally came to me because she had grown a roofing company. We have quite a few roofers at Sarah Jones CPA. Sally had grown her roofing company from about $500,000 to roughly 10 million. She was working with a CPA but did their bookkeeping in-house—we'll talk about that later and why it might not be the best idea. Otherwise, Sally was busy hustling and bustling, growing and going. She would see her CPA once a year.

When Sally decided she was going to sell, she needed a valuation expert. The potential buyers were all requesting audited financials and details, which you need a CPA for. So, when Sally started looking at this, she had a buyer that came to her in the same month that she expressed an interest in getting the valuation done.

The buyer was going to pay far above value because it was a great opportunity, and they wanted to grab it. She had to let that opportunity go because she did not have a CPA who did her bookkeeping. She did not have up-to-date financials for the year. That buyer went to another company that did have all of that information and swooped that opportunity up. It cost Sally a lot of money.

In all three situations, the main issues were the same. There was a CPA who the business owner thought was good, but there was no communication when it mattered. They had requested things, but it wasn't being done. Bottom line, who paid for it? The client did. They missed the opportunity because it was a mismatched CPA relationship with inefficiencies.

The business owners operated out of fear, thanks to a lack of communication. It all lined up with the long-term consequences of staying with the wrong CPA. Do you want to pay hundreds of thousands of dollars in taxes, millions potentially, over a lifetime in taxes or missed opportunities?

You can't afford to have the wrong CPA.

CHAPTER 8

Inadequate Tax Strategies: More Than Just Filing Returns

When it comes to inadequacies, the problem with traditional tax services is that they don't cater to complex wealth. You don't like how the government stewards your money? You need a CPA to help keep it in your pocket and agitate the real cost of generic tax advice on your wealth preservation.

As I've said, we do full-service accounting, tax, and so much more, but by far most referrals I receive are for tax planning. If you just look at the United States, you can find a small tax preparation company at every corner. It's basically a run of the mill McDonald's method of tax preparation. Most of the tax preparers are basically given a three-to-five-week crash course on how to do tax and they have never done tax before.

In fact, if you want to learn a few tricks on how to prepare taxes, you can go to one of these H&R Block or Liberty Tax classes and become a tax preparer—which is pretty scary in my opinion.

Think about it like this: I have hair extensions and I dye my hair blonde. I don't want somebody that has just gone through the training of how to do that. If I'm going to get my eyebrows done, I'm not going to go to somebody that went through training but has no experience or actual license. That's just not how you take care of yourself. You don't trust someone with no experience with things that are important to you.

The same applies here, and we're going to go through the same concepts again and again to demonstrate why.

At a place like that, you say, "Here are my 15 pages, I want you to do my tax return." It's literally all data entry. They're taking the forms and entering the data into the tax return and spitting out a return with no insight, no strategy, and no forward thinking on the part of the tax preparer to think, *Hey, is there a better way?*

Sometimes there's not a better way, because you're looking at taxes from last year. But at least with a good CPA, they will say, "You know what? This year kind of sucks for you. But hey, let's talk. There are a couple things that we could change going forward if we look at tax planning."

That's what you want. You do not want a traditional tax service, especially if you have your own business. If you are doing your own tax return—which I'm assuming you're not if you're reading this book, or you're going to one of those run-of-the-mill tax companies, this goes against everything that we've said already because you need to be working with a CPA.

Let's say that you are already working with a CPA, and you're self-employed. If you're on a Schedule C, you can look at your prior tax return to see if that applies to you, and if you have a sizable net income. If you look at your tax return on line 23 of that 1040, it says *other taxes including self-employment tax.* There's going to be a number there. That's going to tie to your Schedule 2. If you pull that Schedule 2, you can actually look at line four—it will say what you paid in self-employment tax. A lot of CPAs have a client whom they've had for years, and this client has a business, and they still have them filing this way. They still have them paying in that self-employment tax, and they're not telling them how to avoid it.

There's a more efficient way to ask, "Hey, what are your goals? Are you going to grow? What do you think about this?" Tax planning is the highest return on investment that you can get out of a CPA. A CPA will create a roadmap for you. You'll work together now, as you grow, and possibly until you exit and leave the company with your children. It should be a lifetime relationship. Through that relationship, tax planning gets you the biggest bang for your buck and the most savings. It puts you in a place of empowerment.

Why doesn't traditional tax preparation cater to individual strategies or to complex wealth? Because their goal is to crank out as many tax returns as humanly possible, and that doesn't leave time for strategy. That's why we steer you away from those companies and toward a CPA.

As I've said before, CPA's do not learn how to do tax strategy when they go to school. Or when they get that bachelor's degree, or when they take all of those hours and get a master's degree. There's no strategy training that has to be taken before they go sit for the CPA. That is designed to give the end user and our industry a level of knowledge and a benchmark for compliance.

Keeping the taxpayer compliant to GAAP, the Generally Accepted Accounting Principles, does not teach you strategy. It doesn't teach you a lot about how to file tax returns, because you learn that in practice. Your education is meant to make sure you have that knowledge base. A CPA is not enough. You need a CPA who understands, knows, and can implement tax planning strategies for you.

Sometimes I get a tax return, and I look around and wonder, *Who is punking me? Is this a joke? This cannot be a real tax return.* That's how bad they are and why you end up overpaying. There's no clarity. You go through the motion of looking at your tax return and papers. You give it to this person who gives you no communication; there's no insight—they give you this product, and they don't explain it to you. They don't see if you have any questions; you're told to sign, and you have to trust your dollars are going to the IRS. Then you just do that again the next year, without any planning. That's tax life with no clarity.

There's no education with this method. You're getting that tax return at the end of the season, but you're not getting any insight to understand why you're being taxed the way that you are. Sometimes there's literally nothing you can do. Your CPA doesn't show you how it works or why it matters.

All of these issues—the overpaying, the lack of clarity, the lack of education, what it all really results in—gives you a fear-based mentality. Operating through a fear-based mentality is not where you want to be, especially in your finances. When you're in that mindset, you make decisions that are not best for you and your family and your business. You're making them out of fear.

And fear is how money slips through your fingers.

Let's talk about the government for a minute. I'm a US citizen from Texas. I pray things improve, but I will confidently tell you that I am a better steward of my money than the US government is with my money. I'm not saying that we shouldn't pay tax. We have a tax system. It's a requirement. We're going to do everything that we need to do to stay compliant—but I do also feel like you should use the tax code strategically and not overpay in taxes. You need to pay what you're required to pay, but a good CPA knows the code and knows what you can and can't do. They will always keep you above board so you're never in that gray, unlike some tax preparers.

You want to avoid that, but you do want to know the strategies that you can employ to get that tax bill as low as possible. If less money goes to the IRS, that's a little bit more money in your pocket. That way, you can be a good steward of that money. What could that mean? That might mean putting more money into your business. Maybe it's funding your SEP IRA. Maybe it's starting a college fund for your child. Maybe it's starting a brokerage account and getting some of those long-term saving goals. Maybe it's taking a vacation or putting that money aside and purchasing your first home. Whatever that is to you, a good CPA will help you save in tax dollars to keep a little bit of that money so that you can get some of those goals achieved.

What does this look like from a practical perspective? Monthly, I see people come through with all kinds of strange issues, but overpaying in taxes is probably the most common. Even in the off season, a lot of people will come to us just after tax season, and they know they want to make a change. They're proactive about it. I always ask to see the prior year tax return, so I know what's going on.

Last year, I had a new client come in—we'll call her Jane Doe. She has a business, she's a single member, LLC, and she's been this way for about six years. She has a gross income of about $350,000 and she's netting about $120,000 a year. Jane is still on Schedule C, which in tax terms means you're a single member, LLC. That's called a disregarded entity, which goes on your personal tax return via a Schedule C.

Now, Jane Doe has been rocking and rolling. She has a CPA. She came to me, however, because she didn't understand her tax, and she felt like she was overpaying. I went through her tax returns with her and saw that her self-employment tax was significant on her income.

She was overpaying in tax by about $17,000. It was clear on the paper, with very basic math; her CPA had never told her that there was a different way. So, she had just been overpaying in tax, assuming she was supposed to pay that amount without question and assuming that her CPA was handling it all.

When we do free tax analysis for new and potential clients, I always look for that one thing. Are you paying self-employment tax? A lot of people don't even understand self-employment tax because their CPA isn't telling them about it. By far, overpaying in tax is the biggest cost to you when you use a basic tax service or a CPA who does not do tax planning.

I have a thriving tax practice, and we get a lot of tax work, but need the systems and processes in place to make sure that every single person has time dedicated to their return. A CPA needs to do that work and do it well enough to give feedback. If a client doesn't understand their tax return, if there's no clarity there, that client is not going to feel their CPA is doing their job. Once more, the client is the one who ultimately pays for that.

What's the real cost of choosing basic tax preparation? You're the one who pays. It's up to you to make the move to find a strategic CPA. Find a CPA who will give you tax planning, who will give you clarity, who will educate you, and who will make all the difference in the world—and in your wallet.

CHAPTER 9

When Wealth Management Doesn't Manage Wealth

What happens when wealth management doesn't manage wealth? Let's take a look at the problem and the disconnect between wealth management teams and CPA services. I've seen stagnation and a loss of opportunity because of a passive CPA and a wealth management team that didn't work together.

Wealth management is when you have money invested, and you have a stockbroker managing it for you. There are a ton of different brokerages and companies you can go with, but a lot of people will think about companies like Edward Jones or Merrill Lynch or Prudential, to name a few.

There's a lot of companies that will offer insurance, for example, and then offer you wealth management. Wealth management is a great and much needed specialty. The reality is, unless you're an expert, you don't want to manage your own money. You want somebody managing it for you.

But it's the same as the tax side—there is a dark side to tax, and there's a dark side to money management. There are two different structures with wealth management. There's a commission-based structure, and there's an advisory fee, which is a newer format.

Traditionally, when you are a money manager, you're charging an ongoing commission when people buy in. Inherently, there's a conflict of interest. You're supposed to be doing the best thing for the client and for their money and their goals, but you are being paid a commission from the companies based on where you take your clients' funds.

Instead, I recommend you find an advisory. Basically, they're required to be a fiduciary for you and, instead of charging a commission, they charge you a fee. They earn a percentage to manage your funds in the best way for you, for your goals, and for your situation—regardless of what individual firm might be offering X amount of commission. An advisory removes all of that conflict.

However, there is a problem in using a generic wealth advisor.

Let's say you meet this guy who works for Edward Jones. He's probably a great guy, and hopefully pretty smart, but is he the best fit for you? What I often see is when you take a generic, run-of-the-mill financial advisor, and you match them with your CPA. You may have a great CPA, but they're not strategic, they're not communicative, or they're not forward-thinking—all of the things we've already talked about. You put those two together, and you have one of the most frustrating relationships I've seen clients go through.

Why? Let's say that you have a sizable traditional IRA, and you've been told that you should probably look at rolling that over into a Roth IRA, but you need help for the tax implications of it.

I've seen this exact situation many times. So, you go to your financial advisor, and they say, "Oh, well, I can't really give you tax advice. You're going to have to go see your CPA." You go to your CPA, and they say, "Oh, well, I'm not a financial advisor. I can't tell you when to take that out."

The client gets frustrated, then they set up a meeting with the CPA and the financial advisor to come together in one meeting, but neither of them are synergistic in the way that they work. The financial advisor is really just doing what they have to do to get their commission. So, they don't want to do anything extra. On the CPA side, they don't know anything about your investment, so they don't feel like they're able to give advice in any way, shape, or form.

They come together in this meeting, and who pays and is hurt by this lack of synergy? You—the client. You're frustrated, you don't get anywhere, and you have two people on your financial team who are not on the same page. What I recommend is to find a CPA who does the tax planning, who's proactive, and everything else we've talked about, but who also offers wealth management. That's a huge value-add to you as the client. It's a huge piece of synergy, bringing that under one roof. Now you have the same person who knows all of your tax implications, knows your information, your family, and your business goals, in and out. You already know they're educated. They're a CPA and a licensed stockbroker.

In the back of this book, we have a checklist that's going to tell you exactly what to look for in who you hire and how to bring two things into one. If you can bring a CPA and a stockbroker under the same roof, you can have a conversation about strategy and wealth management, and also look at the tax side. It seems impossible to find someone who knows both, but there's been a huge shift with some of my clients when they've prioritized this. There's also usually some cost savings associated with this strategy because otherwise you might pay to meet with your CPA about X, then you have to go have a meeting with your financial advisor about Y. Wouldn't it be nice to have one bill for both?

Bringing these two sides under one roof enables simplicity. A lot of times, especially as you have more money in the market, you reap savings on some of those advisory fees. The problem with generic wealth management is there's no strategy. Just like using a CPA who doesn't do tax planning, you need somebody who does understand wealth management and will give you strategy. Putting that in the same house with a CPA who does tax planning is huge. It can be the difference between hundreds of thousands of dollars over the course of your lifetime.

What about the other major cost? Time suck. We talked about this a little bit, but it's worth revisiting if you're a busy entrepreneur with a business to run. When you have a traditional wealth manager who is commission-based, getting time with that financial advisor is a little difficult. I don't want any hate mail from financial advisors because there are some great financial advisors out there, but I'm talking about the ones who simply don't go above and beyond. Sometimes, it's hard to get a meeting with your financial advisor.

Let's go back to our situation with a traditional IRA that you're trying to roll over into a Roth, or where you want to see if you can do capital loss harvesting at the end of the year after some gains. Is there anything you can do to offset the expense? Sometimes it's difficult to get in with your financial advisor and, once you do, they'll say, "Oh, we're not qualified to make those decisions. You need to talk to your CPA." Then, you go to your CPA, and they say, "Well, I'm not a money manager. I can't give you insight or give you advice on that account. You need to go to your financial advisor." This is a merry-go-round you cannot afford to keep riding.

That frustrating time suck can be eliminated if you work with one person. What kind of CPA do you always want to work with? One that does tax planning and is proactive. You want a CPA who communicates. If you also find a CPA who does wealth management and is qualified, it's a huge game changer.

The SEC regulates the wealth management industry very closely. There are checklists and standards to make sure you're matching your client with the right product. But what I've found is that financial advisors don't always give you a roadmap. Once again, you need a plan. You always start with the end in mind.

For example, if you came to me and said, "Sarah, my goal is to retire with three million dollars in the bank and be able to live off that comfortably by the time I'm 65, okay?" That is what I would use as the basis to create a plan for your wealth. It's based off *your* goals, not Sarah Jones's goals. It's not based off how much commission I would make if I put your money in X accounts.

That's not what it's about. Wealth management is a roadmap for you, for your family, for your business, for your success. You start with the end goal, and then you have somebody go through what that looks like. You say you want three million by the time you're 65, and you're 25 now? What does that look like? What do we need to do to get there in the next 40 years?

From there, we go through all of the compliance and build out the plan together. I've seen many situations where somebody has a financial advisor just hanging out, getting a commission off of them. I'm not saying these are bad guys—I just don't feel like they're the best guys for my clients. I like to see my clients with a CPA who does tax planning and solid wealth management planning all under one roof.

There's a huge amount of synergy. You're going to get a short-term and a long-term plan for success—a good roadmap. You're going to be able to take advantage of any income loss or harvesting, any strategies that are available on an annual basis. You're going to be able to get tax implications and tax strategies. If you had a traditional IRA, and you're wanting to roll it over to a Roth, you're easily going to be able to do that.

I don't want hate mail from financial advisors, but you need to consider finding a CPA who also does wealth management. Having those together in one place is going to bring you more clarity. You're going to have more education. That fear-based mentality is going to disappear. The synergy is going to be a value-add. There will be cost savings when you have things under one roof. It's been a huge game changer for a lot of my clients, and I hope you'll get to experience that shift.

CHAPTER 10

The Missing Pieces

Truth be told, I get a little long-winded when I start talking about the missing pieces, but I'm super passionate about how to avoid working with a CPA who has limited options. You don't want to work with a CPA who only does tax just because you have a need for that. You also need bookkeeping and CFO services. You need coaching, and you need wealth management.

I've seen so many real-life examples of clients who have really suffered and missed out because they haven't worked with a CPA who manages everything they need. What about you? Maybe you're working with a great CPA who just does tax. Remember, I'm not hating on CPAs—just CPAs who aren't good for their clients.

If they're a one-stop shop you can go to, trusting that they're really good and they do everything proficiently, then you just might have what you need. But you do not want a CPA who just does tax.

The first problem with that is what we already looked at, asking, "What is the cost of basic tax services?" You overpay, you have no clarity, you have no education, and you ultimately pay hundreds of thousands of dollars more in unnecessary tax over your lifetime.

You need somebody who's not outdated. You need somebody who's a hustler. You need an entrepreneur who's very like-minded with you. That person should handle your bookkeeping, your CFO, your coaching, your wealth management, and your tax and your tax planning.

In the last chapter we talked about wealth management. Now, we're going to talk about bookkeeping and we're going to talk about CFO services and coaching.

What is bookkeeping? People ask me that all the time. If you have a business, you should have QuickBooks online and you should manage every single transaction that comes in and out of your business. It's extremely important and it's important for a couple of different reasons. Really, from the tax compliance side, your QuickBooks is your ledger. That means that if you get audited, the IRS will potentially want to look at your QuickBooks. That's where all of your transactions, registers, and your financial trail exist. You also need bookkeeping because there's a lot more to it than QuickBooks.

I worked with a pretty large company who did their QuickBooks online in-house. They grossed about 26 million a year, and the owner wanted to continue to do their QuickBooks online to save the cost of professional bookkeeping.

When I did her taxes at the end of the year, her tax preparation bill was always so high because I had to spend hours upon hours just correcting so many of her errors. She would have actually saved money by having a CPA team do her bookkeeping on a regular basis, rather than me going back and cleaning it all up. It's not difficult, but when it's messy, it becomes really difficult and very time consuming.

Why do you need bookkeeping? Because you can't afford not to have it.

Sometimes I'm with a client and I say, "I can send you a report by the 15th of every month showing exactly what you made last month, the state of all your accounts, and seeing everything reconciled. Would that help you run your business?"

Practically, it's extremely useful. If you're trying out a new marketing strategy, how is it actually trending your income? If you're going to use that data to make real-time decisions in your business—which every single person should be doing—bookkeeping is one of the highest returns on your investment.

Having that clarity, that monthly pulse, will help drive your business, and it keeps you in check. We do a lot of bookkeeping, and we have clients using our software. It tells us who opens the reports. Sometimes a client who never opens the report—they just want the books clean. I can respect that, but I think there's a huge amount of value that's just being wasted. You want to get those reports and look at them.

At Sarah Jones CPA, we have a system called Build Protect Grow. We help you build your dreams, protect your assets, and grow your legacy. Build is all about bookkeeping. How do you even know what you're trying to build if you can't see what's going on?

I'm writing this near the beginning of the year, and everybody's talking about New Year's resolutions. Right now, I'm actually sitting in a hotel in London, and it is January 2nd, 2024. So, when I go on Facebook and I scroll, I see all these new diets and gadgets and blah, blah, blah. Let's say that you're wanting a new body, and you want to overhaul your health. Going back to an earlier analogy, it's like hiring a trainer, going on a diet, and never getting on the scale to check your progress.

Think about that. That's what the bookkeeping is for. It gives you insight into what has gone on so you can know if it's good or what you need to change.

Now, why do you need a CPA to do your bookkeeping? I personally know of 10 really good bookkeepers—and they're not CPAs. I am not hating on these people in any way, shape, or form. But if you know very little about the financial industry, having a CPA doing your books means knowing they have a certain level of qualification and they know what they're doing.

Pretend this chapter is the first time you have ever heard of bookkeeping, and you still don't know what it entails. If you wanted to make a website tomorrow and start offering bookkeeping services, you could. There are a lot of companies that do not know what they are doing. I don't know anything about roofing. If a roofer shows up to fix my roof, I'm not going to know if it's a bad job or not. Same thing here. Make sure your bookkeeping is done by a CPA firm. Again, I know a lot of great bookkeepers who aren't CPAs, but going with a CPA ensures they know what they're doing and that you're going to get a certain level of quality work.

At what point should you have bookkeeping and CFO services done? It's a little different for every company, depending on what it looks like in the transaction level, but I will say that once you're making a hundred thousand dollars a year, you need a bookkeeper. Again, a lot of people will say, "I can't afford a bookkeeper." But it's not a full-time employee if you're using a CPA firm like Sarah Jones CPA. We do bookkeeping in all 50 states. We come in through your QuickBooks online and do it in the background. It's a fraction of the cost you would pay to have even a part-time employee, and it's done by a CPA firm. That's what you need to look for.

What about CFO services? A CFO and coaching are both valuable, but they're different from bookkeeping. Bookkeeping gives you clean books, and your bank account and credit cards are reconciled. We do your transactions for you. We give you those reports. Sometimes that might include a monthly meeting to go over questions that you have. You look for trends in the financials.

CFO services are for those higher-level services such as, "I really need help with my cash flow. I really need help with budgeting and achieving goals or getting my team in check and tracking revenues." That's what a CFO service is for.

The biggest thing I do as CFO is really specific coaching. I coach the client one-on-one where we're looking deep into their cash flow. It may be a company that's doing really well, and they want to grow, but they can't get their expenses in check. We go through specific goals, monthly goals that their team has to integrate, and we have a custom-built dashboard that looks at their cash flow and their goals and keeps them in line.

That's what we do. Outside of tax planning, CFO services and CFO coaching is probably the second largest return on investment you can get from a good CPA. What happens when you get to the level where you're making six figures, or even seven figures, and things are really good, but you just don't feel like you have a good pulse on all of your trajectories? What if you're unsure about the KPIs for your teams? A good CFO service, which a lot of good CPAs will offer, can custom-build a framework or roadmap to help you achieve all of those goals.

I see this all the time, but what's the real cost?

If you're using a bookkeeping service, and it's not a CPA, there's a good chance that it's probably not good service, and it's probably not accurate. This isn't always true by any means, but there's a good chance of inaccuracy. I've had to have this conversation with many clients that come over. I say, "Look, I'm going to have to redo all of this work." They've already paid for a service. They were probably trying to save some money. But ultimately, they're going to have to pay all over again for a CPA to do it. Those cleanup projects can be very expensive because they're so time consuming. Being double charged for a service is never fun. A CPA will help prevent that.

But I've also seen where a potential client calls and says, "Hey, we're being approached and we have this great opportunity where we might be able to sell our company, but we don't have books. I don't know what I should do." So, they come to us, and their books haven't been done for three years. That's a huge lost opportunity. For a person who's potentially wanting to buy, hearing that the books have not been taken care of is a huge red flag. Sometimes, that alone will stop their interest. If you are serious about growing your company, growing it to scale it, and to sell it, you need books. You need books every single month, and you need it done by a CPA.

I had a client come to us who wanted CFO coaching. CFO coaching is all based on your bookkeeping. So, if the bookkeeping is crap, the CFO output's going to be crap. Crap in, crap out.

We had to get his bookkeeping completely turned around. He came over as a client at Sarah Jones CPA and, once we had his books clean, we could actually do CFO work. It was a game changer for him.

The whole premise of this chapter is just the missing pieces that come from working with a CPA who has limited options. You need a CPA who does tax planning, bookkeeping, CFO, and wealth management in one house.

If you had your attorney, bookkeeper, tax preparer, insurance agent, and financial advisor all at one table, how difficult would it be to get everybody on the same page? Most people have one person for each thing. When one thing happens, you have to go to each person and get their input.

No, you want a CPA who does everything in one house. That's what we do at Sarah Jones CPA. If you can imagine being at a table with all those financial professionals working together on your behalf, that's extremely valuable for you in getting you where you want to go.

CHAPTER 11

The Frustration of One-Size-Fits-All Financial Advice

D o you get frustrated by one-size-fits-all financial advice? The problem is the lack of personalized service from your current CPA. Time isn't properly set aside for you. You're just a file in a cabinet—talk about missed opportunities!

At Sarah Jones CPA, we're super passionate about systems and processes. After 15 years in this industry, I've used all the experiences, good and bad, to shape my firm. Like I said, in school, you're taught to be compliant. You're not taught how to run a business. You're not taught how to communicate with clients. You're not taught how to do tax planning. You have to figure all of that out on your own if you want to serve clients well. And if you picked up this book, the title resonated with you because you're not happy with your CPA. I can probably guess that you never hear from them and, when you do, you have absolutely no idea what they're talking about. That's what I hear every single day when I meet with new clients. It's not that they had a bad CPA—they're probably a great CPA, they're probably just not a great fit for you. They're not a proactive CPA and don't have systems and processes.

When you go to that run-of-the-mill tax prep CPA—who might have a little strip center set up with a sign saying, *Tax Season*, you won't get what you need.

I'll say this in every chapter, even if you're sick of hearing it: Do not go to some tax strategist or somebody who is not a CPA. You need someone who will make sure you stay above board and will give you the best quality work and education about your finances. You need someone who will shoot straight on what you can and cannot do.

Make sure you use the resources at the end of this book to find a CPA who will give you personalized service.

So, let's avoid the one-size-fits-all concept. What is personalized service? I'll tell you what it isn't. Personalized service is not you taking your tax forms and dropping them off at your CPA office and having the administrative assistant, who is probably very lovely and very friendly, tell you that they'll get back to you.

Let's say that you drop them off on February 1st. You sign your engagement letter. They tell you that it'll get worked on, and they'll give you a call. So, a couple of weeks go by, and you don't hear anything. You call on February 24th. She says, "Oh yeah, we're not working on it yet, but if she has any questions, we'll let you know."

They wait a couple more weeks. Well, now you're getting a little nervous. It's April 1st. You call back and they say, "We're going to have to file you an extension because they weren't turned in on time." You say, "Hey, I turned these into you guys on February 1st." She tells you, "I know, but we're just really backlogged."

That's what exceptional service is *not*. Again, that's not necessarily a bad CPA. They simply do not have systems and processes in place to manage their client workload, and they're going to have frustrated clients. But here's the main problem—who ends up paying for that? You do. You got your stuff in on time, and that should have been plenty of time for them to finish the work.

On the flip side of that, I've had clients literally call my office who are *not* current clients. It's April 12th, and they say, "Hey, we need to drop this off. Can you get this done for us by April 15th?" We say, "No, we cannot." We're very upfront about it. You want a CPA who's upfront about their processes and their systems. For example, we say, "If you want to guarantee that your tax return is done by the deadline, we need the complete set of everything. We need it 30 days in advance." That's generally the standard if we want to offer personalized service.

What else is not personalized service? Let's go back to that same example. On February 1st, you submit all your documents, and they get the tax return done. And let's say that by February 17th, you have a tax return that's sent to you for signature, and you can come pick it up.

So, you're saying, *Great!* You go to the CPA office and have a gazillion forms. You've never even met with the CPA. It says $4,500 is due to the IRS. Here's your voucher to pay. Julie, the very lovely, very kind administrative assistant, cannot answer any of your questions, and you're not able to get in with the CPA because it's the height of the tax season. You have no clarity, no education, and you ask, "Do I pay this? Is it due?"

What you really want is a CPA who has systems and processes in place so that they can give you personalized service, even if they're a large firm. That's the key. You want a good CPA who is in demand, because that means they're good at what they do—but you need to make sure they can accommodate your needs.

Going back to the interview and checklist that you're going to find at the end of the book, it's really important to ask your potential new CPA how they communicate and what their processes are. You want that personalized service, but you need to make sure it matches your expectations.

We want to discuss the impact of lack. Let's talk about some things that happen when you lack personalized service. Probably by far the most common is just overpaying. If you drop your documents off to a CPA and you never hear from the CPA or a tax manager, and you're only working with the administrative person up front, it's a problem. Be wary if there's not a single back and forth email of, "Hey, I've got a question about this," or "Hey, I see something that might be a little bit of a red flag when we file."

It's true that your tax return could be super simple. If you have one W2 and a couple donations, that's pretty straightforward. But at the same time, if you're reading this book, that's probably not you. You probably have a business, or you are a high net-worth individual, and you may have significant documents and forms that are going to their office.

I think the lack of communication from the CPA themselves is a sign of impersonal service. I've seen a lot of situations when new people come and I look at their documents, and they've overpaid on tax and generic services and solutions. If you're a business owner, and you don't understand how you're being taxed, I think that's a red flag. If you cannot get an answer as to why you're being taxed, and if they won't take the time to explain that to you, it's impersonal. If you send an email and ask a question like, "Hey, can you explain to me how my tax bill got computed this year?"

If, instead of responding back and saying, "Hey, let's have a meeting to go over the breakdown," they just say, "Here, you can go to this. It's the IRS table." That's another issue to be aware of.

For me, knowing that the person asking questions doesn't know anything about tax, they're going to need more than just a link to a tax table. That, to me, is a sign of impersonalized service for sure. If you're frustrated during tax season or after tax season, if you don't feel like you understand your tax bill, if you feel like there's no planning, that is a sign of poor service.

These problems really end up costing you. You're the one that pays for them, because there are so many lost opportunities. With personalized service, you're going to be able to take advantage of opportunities, especially if you're talking about and having bookkeeping and your CFO services done. You'll be able to take advantage of opportunities on the fly, because you have the information and resources available. By having no tax planning, you are overpaying in tax. That frustration during tax season will feed into the fear-based mentality. You don't want to be in the place of operating out of fear, because you're going to make decisions that are not the best for you, for your company, and for your family.

CHAPTER 12

The Strategic CPA – A New Financial Ally

I t's time to talk about the strategic CPA—your new financial ally.

Up to this point, we've considered all the reasons why you should fire your CPA and the signs and stories about what you should look out for. But now, we're really going to shift into the much-needed clarification of what you actually need. This is your roadmap for success in navigating your search. Finding the strategic CPA is like the first bite of cake. You never knew that you needed a strategic CPA, someone who will save you a crap ton of money. They will give you a roadmap for success, and we're going to talk about those words I won't stop talking about.

They're going to give you clarity, education, and help you to not operate in fear.

So, what is a strategic CPA? What is their role as your advisor? To answer, I'm going to give you a big brain dump.

They're going to have systems and processes in place to accommodate all of their clients and their needs and be able to clearly communicate those systems and processes. At Sarah Jones CPA, if you call right now and say, "Hey, I need to talk to Sarah," you will not get me on the phone. I time-block every single day and everybody is asked to make an appointment on my calendar link.

If I'm in the middle of preparing your tax return, and I have a potential or current client randomly call me for a question, I don't think you would appreciate it if I stopped what I was doing and take a random call, then get back to your tax return. I'm going to respect your time and mine enough to have everything time-blocked. Whatever I'm doing, I'm a hundred percent there.

That's what you want. You want a CPA who knows and understands. You want someone who builds their time and calendar appropriately. Your CPA should not have high staff high turnover. There are people who come to me and say, "I really liked my CPA, but as he grew, I started working with the staff and, every single year, I got a new staff member on it. They wouldn't know my info and I'd have to re-explain it every year. I got sick of that. There are mistakes that we have to go through every year."

You want a CPA with staff that's built a family-style culture. You really want a team that's been there for a long time. That's an indicator of good leadership, of good people, and as a client, you're going to enjoy working with that team. You want a CPA who will grow with you. You want a CPA who is proactive and does everything you need, someone who will accommodate you.

Let's say that you start a business, and you find a CPA. At first, it's a really great fit, but then you start growing, and it's too much and they can't accommodate you anymore. Now you're stuck and you have to find a new CPA. You want a CPA who can grow with you. Maybe at the very beginning they're just keeping you compliant with your annual tax, but two or three years down the road, you need help with bookkeeping. And then a couple years later, you need CFO services. Then, you need tax planning, and now you need wealth management planning. You need a CPA who will be able to do all of those pieces for you and help you throughout your life's journey in one spot.

Again, when you do that, there's synergy and you actually end up saving money because everything happens under one house. If you're going for bookkeeping services, you need those monthly reports. You need monthly meetings for CFO services, and you need cash flows and goals. You need an analysis and monthly accountability for wealth planning. You should have a roadmap for success. You should have an advisory, somebody that is a fiduciary that is not being paid on commission. You need a succession plan. You need long-term success on tax and tax planning.

You need a dedicated team. You do not want the H&R Block business plan. Again, you must use a CPA for this. Like we talked about, qualified tax planning is the number one return on your investment—you will save hundreds of thousands of dollars over your lifetime with proper tax planning. If you are not having tax planning done, you are missing out as a business owner.

Your new financial ally is the strategic CPA. Everything that we've talked about, they will do for you. They handle everything from the beginning of the book, where we talked about problems and inefficiencies and a lack of strategy. The right CPA will replace all of those issues with the good stuff. You will have clarity, you will have education, you will have savings, you will have synergy, and you'll be operating out of place of empowerment to run your business, your home, and your family. Avoid the fear-based mentality. Find a CPA who works for you.

CHAPTER 13

Custom-Tailored Tax Planning for the Affluent

We have certainly touched on many concepts so far, but it's time to dive a little deeper, starting with custom-tailored tax planning for the affluent. We're going to consider tax planning, advanced tax planning, and strategies and examples of wealth enhancement to save on taxes and what you should be looking for.

The biggest return on your investment with working with a CPA is tax planning. Now, not all CPAs are created equal, and not all CPAs do tax planning. We've said this before, and I'm going to beat it into you many times. You need a CPA who does tax planning, because over the cumulation of your lifetime, it could mean the difference between paying hundreds of thousands of dollars extra in tax or saving hundreds of thousands of dollars in tax and having that money in your pocket. You can use that money to invest back into your business or to start your business. You can use it for that new startup you wanted or to put money in your retirement savings. You can even simply take that vacation you've been wanting to take.

I'm not saying that tax planning is free or that tax planning is the same or included in tax preparation. Tax planning is absolutely a separate and additional service to tax preparation. When you go to get your taxes done, Sarah Jones CPA does tax preparation. I automatically look when I've done the tax return. Even if it's a new client, I go through that process. Often, someone comes to me as a new client in February or March, and I have to remind them that we can't do stuff for the prior year. But moving on, it's getting it done. We're making sure that it's accurate and we're compliant, but at the end of that process I will say, "Hey, I really see some opportunity for tax planning. Why don't you book a consult with me, and let's talk about what tax planning looks like?"

I'm saying that all to say tax planning is not free and it is not included with tax preparation. It's completely separate and, to be honest, it is typically not a cheap service. Tax planning is a high value service. It's very custom and specifically built out for every single client—it's individualized. So be prepared to spend a good chunk of money for some good tax planning.

What does the tax planning process look like? It typically starts with a free or complimentary review, a tax analysis, and that means the number one thing I'm referred for is tax planning. The potential client will call, and they say, "Hey, I was told that you're the best, and that I need to talk to you. I just feel like my taxes are high. I want to see what I can do to save some money." That's a good place to start to see if they're a candidate for that.

If it's somebody who's local, they will come in and drop off their tax returns. Since we are licensed in all 50 states, and we deal with clients all over the country, we give non-local clients access to our secure portal online. You want a CPA to look at your prior year tax returns—every single tax return. If you have multiple businesses and entities, they need all of the business returns, and then your personal return. You want to make sure they have the full picture. You want the CPA to look at everything you have.

They might ask a couple of clarifying questions, and they also should ask about your goals, both short-term and long-term. That can come into play with the planning process, and you want to make sure that it's a really good fit. They're going to make recommendations and you want those to fit with your goals, which sometimes is not quantified on a tax return.

What are we looking for? I'm looking at everything, just like we talked about. What do you have and how is it all pieced together?

I also want to see how much you paid in tax and what tax bracket that you're in. I specifically want to see if you're paying anything that's unnecessary, like self-employment tax. I'll look at how efficient your current system and tax set up is. And, again, I want to have that conversation with you about your current and your long-term goals.

From there, I will put together a plan with a proposal of savings. I would say, "Hey Mr. Joe, thanks so much for sharing this with me. Here is your proposal. I propose that if we engage in tax planning, we could put something together with these kinds of processes and steps. It would save you 25% on average per year." From that point, your CPA will send you an engagement letter, which means, "Hey, based on the proposal, this is what we're going to engage together to do." It should give you a timeline of how long the process should take. It will give you an estimated price of that tax plan in terms such as you both agree for that tax agreement. After the engagement letter is signed, typically the CPA will send you an invoice for the tax planning.

Once that invoice is handled, the CPA will get to work. For my clients, I'll actually develop the plan and put it together. I will then deliver the plan to you and typically ours will come with a formal tax memorandum. That way, when you have questions, you have a tangible reference guide.

I like to use an example to illustrate this. If you're not sleeping one night and you have a question about your tax plan, you might shoot me an email. But most of the time, you're not going to actually reach your CPA at midnight. The memorandum is your tangible reference guide for things as they come up.

After you have your plan and memorandum and everything is signed, we will set up a meeting to go over all of the tax planning that we've set up. We'll make sure that you fully understand everything, and then we will actually implement it.

There is another piece of this, however. A lot of people who engage with us for tax planning think getting the tax planning implemented and done and developed is where it ends. But that's not the case. You still need to touch base with that CPA. It is not a one and done. If you have those strategies implemented, that's great. You're going to have some great tax savings and you have those strategies there, but you still need to check in with your CPA.

It's best to communicate with your CPA quarterly. That's my default. I think that's long enough apart to where those calls aren't going to be redundant, but it's close enough together that if there is anything new, nothing's going to fall through the cracks. It gives you enough pulse throughout the year that you're always being proactive. There might be things that come up that you don't even know you need to talk about with your CPA, but one of those quarterly calls that come up and you remember, "Oh, this is something we need to talk about." It gives you that opportunity.

What I really want to stress here is that for your continued success, you need to touch base and continue to have the ongoing communication with your CPA. Maybe what you set up as a plan works. But maybe over the next five years, your income goes up 200%. It might mean that your tax planning still works, but maybe there are new things you will need to implement. You might need to do stuff a little bit differently. You're not going to know that if you're not having those pulse points with your CPA.

But at Sarah Jones CPA, we lead by example. So, let's talk about a couple of success stories. As I said, the number one thing that I'm referred for is tax planning services. We do a lot of tax planning for a lot of different people and a lot of different industries. One industry that's super popular right now is for various real estate investors getting involved with tax strategies. The complications of real estate brings us back to an earlier point. Remember we talked about following tax 'experts' on social media and making sure they're qualified? Make sure it's a CPA or a tax attorney.

There are a lot of people on social media right now who are not qualified. They say they're tax strategists or tax specialists, and they're giving awful advice, and they don't know the tax code. Real estate investors have a ton of different rules and regulations and potential loopholes. Because of how complex these rules are, I'm not going to go into these rules that can change before this book is even published. If you're in real estate, if you have short or long-term rentals, if you have properties, or if you're flipping anything either exclusively or alongside your other businesses, you need to get with a CPA who does tax planning. There are a lot of potential things that you can do and a lot of them are going to come into play based on how you participate, what you actually do, and how much your income is.

Sometimes your adjusted gross income will limit certain options, but you need to get with a CPA who knows those rules. Huge, huge savings are available to you.

I had one real estate investor who, because of how he participated in his business and because of how his income fell that year, was able to take a substantial amount of losses to actually have bonus depreciation on improvements. He managed to completely get rid of his tax bill for that year, which was great.

Another thing we do is look at and work with specific business owners on using depreciation rules in certain years. Again, these rules change every single year, so I'm not even going to say, "Hey, you can take X amount of depreciation," because I have no idea when you're reading this book, and that advice might change by the time you're reading this book. These are great incentives for business owners to use, and ultimately the IRS uses these to stimulate the economy.

The IRS wants you to buy things to input more money into your business to spur the economy. By doing so, you get a great potential write-off for these purchases, so there are some rules and regulations on what you can and can't do with them, and it has to be certain asset classes that qualify for this. A good CPA who does tax planning can put that together for you and create a proposal of how you can use bonus depreciation. I have, many, many times, used bonus depreciation to get a client to a zero-tax bill when they have years of really investing in their business. We use these depreciation rules to their benefit, and it's been a great savings for them.

When I initiate tax planning, the very first thing I look at is whether or not they are paying self-employment tax. It's a low hanging fruit. I always call it the silly tax or the stupid tax—not that I feel that the taxpayer is stupid. I feel like it's stupid to pay the self-employment tax because with just a little bit of proper planning, you can avoid that tax and really get a much more efficient bang for your tax buck there. I usually manage to save a significant amount for new and potential clients that come to me, literally every week, when we do an analysis and work on mini tax plans.

Another thing that we look at is to get rid of that self-employment tax is to do that S-Corp election. I know you hear about this from those people that you're following on Facebook and Instagram that do tax.

You hear that and see it, but an S-Corporation can be detrimental and catastrophic in certain instances. If you have a 100% LLC and you're never going to have a partner, an S-Corp is probably a great choice for you. If you have partners involved in an S-Corp, it can be so detrimental because you give up a lot of flexibility and partnership law when you do that S-Corporation election. So, in instances like that, where we have partnerships, or if I have a client that has multiple businesses and different streams of income going on, it does not make sense to do an S-Corp election on all these different entities.

Sometimes we will set up a parent company. In saying this, I'm not giving a ton of details on purpose—I've had the experience of telling somebody they can do this, and they go to an attorney and set something up, but they have no idea of what to ask for, and they do it incorrectly, causing all kinds of issues.

If you want an advanced setup and a parent or a management company to get the tax benefits and the asset and liability protection, you need to find a CPA to look at your information to give you a free consultation. Then, they can custom build you a plan and explain to you why you're doing what you're doing. Those advanced setups can be a huge, huge asset to you and really simplify your business ventures as you start and continue to grow and do different things. But you're also going to get those tax benefits and savings with some extra asset and liability protection. Again, tax planning is the biggest return on your investment. You need a CPA who does tax planning and one who will make you a roadmap for your success.

CHAPTER 14

Integrating CPA Expertise into Your Financial Team

This chapter is all about integrating a CPA and CPA expertise into your current financial team. The solution we're talking about is how the right CPA, that proactive, licensed, tax planning CPA, can bring synergy to your financial team. This allows holistic management, to where you're getting everything in one, and it meshes with your team. When you have clarity and synergy, there's a huge return on your investment. That makes me excited—and it should make you excited too, especially if you've been working with a CPA who is not proactive and does not communicate and is not part of your team. It is a huge difference.

So, as you're navigating this, your CPA should be a member of your team. They should be seen as an extension of your team.

Honestly, you should want to send a Christmas card and a fruitcake to your CPA. It should feel, naturally, like they're on your team, helping you grow and helping you navigate this business roadmap alongside you. The right CPA will bring synergy to your entire team in every area, and I think that the best way to explain this is just to go through the process of how our team works in what we do.

To give you an understanding of what I mean, especially if you're coming into this chapter having never experienced a CPA like that, it's going to be really hard for me just to give you a checklist of *this is what they should do*. I want to explain the emotions and feelings so you can understand the power of having a CPA as part of your team and how they will help every area of your business.

Let's say you have a CPA who is old school, not proactive or communicative, but a once-a-year type person. Then, let's say you have a financial advisor like that, and those two people are not talking to each other. Then, you have an attorney you use once a year to update your board meeting minutes and all of that stuff. Imagine replacing all of those people with one—I'm going to say it again—licensed CPA who does all of that under one roof. The nucleus of everything is you and your business. You are the common denominator. Everybody in that CPA office is coming together as one on your behalf.

It's kind of like your own little mastermind table with all of these professionals working for you for your benefit, okay? That's why it's worth it to have an all-in-one expert. Again, I'm not talking about working with a financial expert that says they do tax, but they're not a CPA. No, you need a CPA.

Now, once you have that person, you want to make sure they are in all facets of your business. So, if you're a business owner, they need to be doing your bookkeeping.

One specific client I have is great. I consider him a really good friend, and we joke about this now on the other side of it, but at the beginning of his business, he was really trying to be a good steward of his money, which I fully, fully support. He got a bookkeeper from India, and I told him, "Hey, I don't think this is a great idea. I'm not saying he isn't a good bookkeeper, but if you ever need any financial statements or due diligence, no CPA is going to use the work of an overseas bookkeeper, and you're going to have to have your work redone." He was like, "Oh, I don't think that's going to come up." I was like, "Okay, whatever you want to do." So, he did this. And then, he got a huge offer for his company.

I had to go back, as a CPA, and redo all of that work. I will tell you, his bill for me to go back and do all of that work, because it all had to be redone—and redone in a time crunch, was $12,000. We've talked about this many times. He'll say, "You were so right. You should have just done it from the get-go." Now, in all of his businesses, he has us do his bookkeeping as a licensed CPA firm because that's very, very important. So, make sure you have a CPA firm doing your bookkeeping. It adds huge checks and balances. It's great for internal controls to have that separation there. But it also brings you clarity.

Having us do all of your bookkeeping, reconciliations, and monthly reports gives you the insight to your business that you need—and you can do different levels of this. You can say, "Oh, I just need clean books. Just send me my reports once a month." Or you could say, "Hey, I want to have just a basic financial meeting once a month." Or "I really want insight. I want custom KPIs. I want a dashboard. I want you to talk to me about my cash flow." You can get a good CPA. We'll custom build that and put it in your engagement on autopilot for whatever you need. Okay?

Let's move on to goal creation and budgeting. Having someone there for synergy in all of your management can help in a number of ways. Maybe your department heads have goals and budgets and need that accountability.

That makes me so excited, because we've gone through this process with some of our clients—especially some of our bigger clients—that have people designated for certain departments. This will actually keep them accountable because the data will help to do that. It takes the emotion out of it. It's not you saying, "Bob, you're sucking in your department." Instead, you can say, "Here's your goal. Here's what we were supposed to meet. Here's where we actually are. Let's actually talk about it. Can we hit this? Where are we missing the mark and how can we improve?"

This is a huge game changer for your business. On the bookkeeping side, having us with your team to manage AR and AP, your accounts receivable and your accounts payable, means that you're going to collect your money faster. I don't even have to explain why that's a good thing.

Everybody wants that. On the AP side, by managing that effectively and paying more strategically, if we know the terms and when things are due, paying as late as we can to take advantage of any discounts is a huge strategy in cash flow and monitoring that AR and AP and the ins and outflows. Most importantly, by having a huge great strategic CPA team as part of your team will help you to actually make decisions in your business in real time. What's really important here is that you have the data on the fly, so it can be pulled. You can make those decisions. If there's an opportunity, you don't have to wait for answers before you jump. I've had a lot of clients who previously struggled when an opportunity would come up that was out of the ordinary. Sometimes it's an anomaly. It's a once in a lifetime opportunity.

Without that data, you have no idea if you can actually pull the trigger on it or not, and sometimes it's too late. If you have one of those CPAs in the background who you talk to once a year and you say, "Hey, I actually need all of this stuff updated, and I need it done today," you know what happens? They charge you an arm and a leg because it's a ton of work. It's a bottleneck for them. It takes them forever to do it, and it's the most frustrating experience in the world. Having a CPA firm do your bookkeeping and being a part of your team as a holistic strategic team year-round, means that you can make decisions when you need to on the fly. You have all of your decisions and your financial information available for you.

And now, let's talk about CFO services from this perspective. For my clients who are making seven figures, it's time to at least have an introduction call to see if it makes sense to talk about, not only bookkeeping, but true CFO coaching. What I'm talking about with a CFO coach is all about what bookkeeping is. We're going to keep you clean and compliant and give you the data that you need to run your business. A CFO comes in and says, "Okay, you've already got all that. You're organized. You got all the details you need. What are your specific goals and how are we going to get your cash flow there to achieve X goals?"

They keep you accountable, giving you a custom dashboard based on your custom goals for your business and the key drivers that actually blow the lid off your goals. They have the accountability to call you out on your crap if you're not doing it. If, for example—and I've had this happen—a client says, "We need to grow gross revenue by 25% this year."

We're going to track that every single month and break it down. If we're not building that revenue, we're going to have an unemotional conversation, without pointing fingers. It's a data-driven conversation based around your goals, your templates, and us guiding you with the accountability that you need to go achieve such goals.

Now, I want to give you three examples of how our team, Sarah Jones CPA, works as a holistic, synergistic, proactive, gung-ho CPA team. I'll show you how we've come in for three different clients. I am changing the names, of course, for client confidentiality, but we'll look at how this process has overhauled their businesses.

So, the first company is a large roofing company we have helped up north in two different states. They've since then merged and done all kinds of different things. When they came to us, they were absolutely a one-man show.

He did a great job, but he was working *in* his business. He was not a business owner. He was a worker in his own business. He partnered with somebody else who was strategic and would do backend ops and things like that, which is amazing, but he had no financial background. We were really pivotal in working with him as a holistic, synergistic team to get stuff set up. For example, before they came to us, they had manual timecards.

It's not 1985.

We got their payroll system set up to where the guys could actually clock in and out on their phones. This was GPS coordinated so that everything could be tracked, and you could actually cost payroll to each job where the guys were. It was a huge, streamlined process for them. Before, they were doing manual invoicing, so we got all their invoicing and all of their products and services set up on QuickBooks for them.

We helped them manage that AR and collect payments before their AP. They had a stack of bills they'd go through once a month. They had no idea what was due and what the true cost was per job, so we overhauled that. We got set on all their vendor accounts. We could track those accounts per job. We could actually look at job costing and see every single job they did. We saw revenues that came in, all of the overhead costs, all of the payroll and direct labor costs, all of the direct cost of goods sold, and what they actually made per job. We overhauled their operations and gave them streamlined processes. Through that, they were able to transform and grow their business.

They started this three-year relationship at around 1.5 or 2 million. This last year, they grossed about $10 million. It was a great overhaul in streamlining with a synergistic CPA who really helped them to grow their business.

Another client is in the manufacturing field. They use a completely different CRM for all of their stuff, so they created a widget for upstream oil. We helped them streamline their reporting. They had no way to track some of their open orders because they weren't coming over to QuickBooks. We were able to pull that reporting and get it automated so we could pull it and send it every single Friday. It was ready for them every Monday when they had their department meetings. Everything completely changed. Just that one aspect of thinking outside the box and seeing what our client needed meant coming alongside them as their strategic partner, their synergistic and holistic CPA—we are a part of them.

We're an extension of them and that enables us to overhaul and increase their productivity.

I don't have a favorite client, but let's look at one near the top of the list. He is a serial entrepreneur, all over the place, with a heart of gold. He had so many different revenue streams and businesses going on and he had no clarity at all. We came alongside him and became his CPA, his tax accountant, but also his bookkeeper and CFO Team. We integrated and got all of his stuff under one banner. We took over all of his workflow for all of his businesses.

Our team got that handled. We got him through the onboarding process, got him clean, got to the point where we were very quickly doing his transactions weekly, categorizing everything, doing his payroll, and giving him monthly reports. We started out with a monthly report and monthly meeting to go over the report. Once he understood the reports and what this balance sheet said, with profit and loss, we custom created a budget.

I hate the word budget, but it was a roadmap for him that showed all of his businesses in one and the cash flow of each business. He saw everything that was going on and it gave him an immediate, high-level view of everything. One—it gave him clarity. Two—it took away that fear-based mentality of not knowing what's going on. Three—most importantly, we integrated a weekly meeting with him and his department heads to review this custom-based KPI scorecard with this data for him to drive their goals.

Everybody got on board the first couple of months. I don't feel like some of his department heads liked the process, but they got on board because they started to see the power and the clarity that they got from that data. It brought everybody together in a tangible way that was not emotional. It was data-driven, and everybody knew what their goals were. Everybody started rowing the same direction in that boat. We transformed them and their company by giving them clarity.

So, a good CPA will do this. A good CPA should be seen as an extension of your team, and you want them involved in everything. There's such power in having a CPA who does everything for you under one roof. It will absolutely drive your business, give you clarity, take away that fear-based mentality, and enable you to crush your goals.

CHAPTER 15

Finding Your CPA Match – The Selection Process

So, now we come to the point of implementing the change. You picked up this book because you recognize that your CPA sucked—otherwise you wouldn't be reading a book called *Fire My CPA*. You understand the why, and what the problems are. We've probably agitated your emotions a little bit and figured out why you feel the way that you feel. It's warranted. And now, we've gone through what you should be looking for— that strategic, communicative, tax planning CPA. You're looking for someone who is a true implementation and an extension of your team. So, how do you actually do this? How do you search at this point? Yes, you need to fire your CPA. You know what you're looking for. But how do you actually go about finding a CPA? What does the selection process look like?

In this chapter, we're going to go through some step-by-step processes as a guide to helping you find and vet out a CPA who understands your needs. I equate this to when you find a doctor, like we've illustrated. You want to work with this doctor because there's synergy and there's value there. When you have a doctor who knows your medical history, your family history, and you work together, it's a good strategy short-term. But you're also together for the long-term because there's a lot of value and benefit there. So, finding a CPA is a little bit like a dating process. I've not dated in a long time. That would be a very scary process, but it's the same concept. You want to make sure that it's a great fit for both of you.

You want to test the waters a little bit. You need to go look at a couple different CPAs and go through this process. You don't want it to be like the dating process, where you get married really quick, you get divorced, and you have an ex-spouse. You don't want that, okay? It's hard. It's frustrating to go through and it creates more work and more costs for everybody.

Do your due diligence. If you know that you need a new CPA, go find a couple and go through this process. Really take the time. Don't just jump into it.

First, before you even look at anybody externally, or any other CPA, I want you to look at you. I want you to look at your values, your goals, your communication styles, and your expectations. I will put a disclaimer in here: You need to make sure your expectations are realistic. For example, you cannot say, "I expect a CPA to respond within an hour." Your CPA is not your full-time employee. That's not going to happen. You need to look at your expectations at the cost versus the service level of what you're doing,

You need to look at your ability to be open, coachable, and honest with yourself. As a CPA I'll remind you this relationship is coming together fueled by finances. There is inherently an aspect of fear that we're going to have to overcome together. If, the second that something goes wrong or comes up with your CPA, you're immediately pointing your finger about something that is really your own fault, that is not going to work. I'm going to be open and honest with a client who does that and say, "Hey, you know what? I really would love to have a conversation with you, but I'm going to need you to be open and take some accountability here. Here are seven emails where I've asked you for this and you never responded once. That's why your tax return is not ready— I've asked you for this seven times."

Taking a little bit of accountability in that process is really pivotal, okay? After you've done that, after you have looked at yourself and how you like to communicate your expectations, what you're looking for, your values, and your goals, then I want you to write down what your ideal CPA relationship looks like. Get out a piece of paper or if you want, or use the back of this book, and write down some notes. I'm going to give you some prompts, okay? Clear communication channels, a rockstar team, a one-stop shop, a CPA who does tax planning, communication expectations, average response time, and here's the last thing that we're about to go into: price is not a factor.

If you picked up this book, you're probably a business owner doing a sizable amount of business. A lot of times, if you're not a business owner doing a sizable amount of business, you typically don't have a CPA. You're using TurboTax, going to H&R Block, things like that. By picking up this book, there's a good chance that you're a business owner and you have a certain level of net worth. What I'm getting at here is that price is not a factor in who you should look for. Cheapest is absolutely not the best. I truly believe you need to be a good steward of your money, and I fully support that. Cheap is not good value. Your CPA should be seen as a huge return on your investment, a valuable partner in your overall team, not simply a price.

You shouldn't shop. Sometimes we get a call, and it's a potential client that says, "What are your prices?" I can tell that that is not the client for us. It's not that we're expensive—we're very in line with most other CPAs—but I know that their mindset is off, and it's not a client that's aligned with our values. Between price and needs, price is a liar.

After looking at yourself, go through that process of writing down what your ideal CPA relationship looks like. Put that in a little paragraph so that when we get to the further step of actually going to look at some CPAs, you can share that with them, and you can tell really quickly if y'all are a good match or not.

We are going to come back to price, but that's something that you're going to ask at the very end, after you have looked at CPAs. You're really just doing it to make sure that it's not something astronomical and way outside of your budget.

The third step is to reach out to some CPAs and do a consult. Now, I would say probably the most impactful way to get a referral from a CPA is to go on social media. Ask people that you trust. If you get people that you wouldn't take a recommendation from in other areas of your life, take it with a grain of salt. But you can also go on Google and look for *CPAs near me*, or if you're looking for somebody local or CPAs who do tax planning, search for them. Look at who you trust and ask them for a referral or check Google and look at reviews before reaching out.

We want to do consults. You want to take your ideal CPA relationship statement with you and maybe bring your prior tax returns so you can go through it, but you want to do a consult no matter what. How many CPAs should you look at? It depends on you. I think that you at least need to look at two or three. I think you don't need to go over five or six. You're going to know as you go along. If you get a handful of CPAs and talk to them, out of those, you're going to have a good feel. I think some of them are going to quickly be those CPAs who you're going to find that aren't proactive, and you're going to see that with them not openly talking about tax planning and ideas and how they communicate.

Then you get that CPA who does talk about, "Hey, we've got these clear communication channels. This is how we operate." When you find somebody that's like-minded with you, you're going to know who the right CPA is for you. Start with three CPAs and see how the relationship feels.

Now, I will be very honest with you. Most CPAs charge for a consult. If you were going to go see a doctor, you paid to go for a professional's time. Most CPAs charge for their time, and from my standpoint, when we did free consults, a lot of people would not show up. They weren't vested. You want to work with people that respect your time. It really has nothing to do with what we're charging for the consult.

It's about making sure that the people are respectful of your time and your schedule, and likewise, we would give you that same respect—so be prepared to pay for it.

At the end of this book, we are going to have a checklist that you can actually take with you to these consults so you can ask them specific questions. It'll have a system so you can actually rate them, but the biggest thing is making sure that you share your expectations are and what you're needing.

Let's say that you've gone and seen four CPAs, and you could tell really quickly that two of them weren't that strategic CPA you're really looking for. The other two you really liked, but one kind of stands out.

What I would suggest you do is follow up with both of them and say, "Hey, I really enjoyed speaking with you. Can you let me know next steps? Like what your average cost is, how to get started with you?" This is the point where you look at their price structure. If they're both great, and if there's a huge difference, absolutely be the best steward of your money. Go with the one that's a little bit more affordable, but only if you like both of them. You don't look at price first. You look at price last. We're just wanting to make sure that it's in your price range, and it's not astronomical.

A good average for hourly rates for a CPA is about $250 an hour for consults, at the time I'm writing this. Tax planning is typically a custom-based fee.

I'm kind of hesitant to give national averages for tax return work, because it varies so widely, but I will tell you that much of this info can be found at aicpa.org. Every single year, they post studies of average tax return rates based on different complexities, and it is a pretty good range for different things. That's what I look at just to make sure that we're in line with industry averages and standards.

So, look at you first—your values, what you need, your expectations, and be prepared to be coachable, honest, and be accountable to a CPA in a long-term relationship. Write down your ideal CPA relationship and take it with you. Go on Google. Ask those you trust around you. Go see at least three CPAs, maybe even up to five CPAs. Then pick the one you want to work with. Follow up with them with your intent of wanting to work with them, how to get started, and then make sure you do ask average fees just to make sure that there's not a surprise.

Price is the least important, but it is still important. You want to make sure you want to be with this CPA, and that you mesh. Now, as you grow, as you need different things, that's really, really important. I cannot tell you how much. A great CPA is huge, and they should be seen as a part of your business, as an extension, as a long-term partnership. If you use the checklist at the end of this book and these tips that we're doing, I'm really confident you can find that CPA who is an extension of your team. That is a strategic and holistic CPA solution for you.

CHAPTER 16

Transitioning to a New CPA - Managing the Shift

This chapter is all about transitioning to a new CPA and managing that shift. We are going to go through what you should do moving forward.

In the previous chapter, we went through how to actually navigate and try to find as new CPA. If you've gone through and used the checklist and did that process, that's great. But before we actually do that, I do want to double check to make sure we're extending that olive branch.

Did you make sure that you first went to your current CPA and make sure they know you're wanting to move on? Is there anything to do to salvage the relationship? Was there a miscommunication?

I say this with a grain of salt, because if you picked up this book, you wanted to fire your CPA. You knew it wasn't a good fit, but at the same time, is it worth double-checking and giving the benefit of the doubt? Just have a quick conversation, if nothing more, when you leave. In a kind and respectful way, you're giving them some feedback they can actually integrate and put into their practice to help other clients so they can give better service.

So, extend that olive branch. Just double-check and say, "Hey, can we have a quick chat? I feel like we're not communicating. I feel like I've tried, and maybe I feel like the communication isn't there. I feel like things take a long time. Is there anything that I can do on my side to help you to make sure that this relationship can continue? Can we integrate some tax planning?"

"Can you guys be my one-stop shop? Can y'all do all of our bookkeeping and all of our CFO work? Because that's what I'm looking for—I'm really looking for a CPA to take those next steps and go with me long-term on this roadmap to success. I want to make sure that both my short-term and my long-term goals are met, and I really want to make sure that I'm aligned with a CPA who is a good fit. Do you think that I am a good fit for you?"

Put it in their court. Then they may say, "Oh no, I don't do tax planning. I don't do any of that stuff. I think you need to find somebody else." Or it could be that there was some miscommunication and maybe they do offer all those services, and it's worth seeing if this CPA relationship is salvageable. If so, if you've extended this olive branch to them, I would say use that same checklist we talked about. Go through those questions with your current CPA, do the same process, and then you can compare them to the CPAs who you've talked to and see where they stand. Maybe through that process you're like, "Hey, I really wish I would've done this two years ago. I think this is a good relationship, and I think we can make it work."

Then, you guys will be on the same page with communication and expectations and deliverables. But maybe you're saying, "Sarah, I know it's not a salvageable relationship. I don't want to extend the olive branch." Or maybe you did and through that, you gave them some really good feedback where you felt like they may have fallen short, in a respectful way. It will give them room to grow in their own business as a business owner. But you know that you want to fire your CPA and proceed. This is what you do.

One, you're going to engage with the new CPA for services. You asked their price last just to make sure it was something in your price range. They will have responded back with what their process is. So, whatever their process is, you follow. They're probably going to put you in their portal. "Here's our engagement letter. We're going to engage for X services."

Maybe they're going to be that all-in-one that we talked about, and they're going to do your bookkeeping, tax, tax planning, and CFO coaching. There will be different engagement services and levels of service engagement for each of those, which they will send to you, and you will go over that together. Now, I will tell you, when you get an engagement letter, they said, "Okay, well tell us what you're wanting."

We do everything with processes and systems in place to make sure we can accommodate our clients' needs. So, whatever you ask for is what you're going to get as far as delivery. If you want bookkeeping and you say, "I want a monthly report and a once-a-month meeting," that means they have time allocated for that. That means if you start expecting a weekly meeting, that's not in the workflow or the price, so then you have to revisit the engagement terms to include the new meeting schedule. Whatever the engagement terms are, that's what will be built out to serve you.

So, make sure that you go through those processes to know what you need, and this is what you don't need. This way the price is accurate to your needs and, more importantly, you know exactly what to expect. The CPA has that on their workflow, so they always make sure it gets done.

What about the day of change? When and where should you switch your CPA? I always say that if you have payroll or W2 employees, it depends. If you're in QuickBooks online, that's a simple change because you're new CPA would just be brought into that. But if you're changing payroll systems or you have to change to their CRMs and software, January 1st is a really good day to change, but that does not also mean that if it's February, you should wait all year. So, if it's later in the year, we've actually kept payroll in the same system and changed everything else over to a more efficient system. We kept the same payroll, though, for the last part of the year and switched payroll over on January 1st. You want to make sure you work with your new CPA to get it figured out.

They will know exactly what you have, and they will give you the best plan of action to make sure that any changes you make are efficient and not as frustrating as they sometimes can be. Payroll can be frustrating to change because it's a lot, and it's date specific. So, navigating that with a CPA who's good at onboarding is key. But, outside of the time constraint of payroll, it's really your preference. I've had some clients that say, "I know my CPA is not a great fit. They're getting towards retirement age. I want to switch, and I'm going to finish out this year with my CPA and I'd like to move to you for next year." Communicate that with your new CPA.

The worst time to move over to a CPA is April 1st, or right before a huge deadline, because at that point, you're coming into a system during a high-level time.

You want to move over around January, when it's fresh, and all the tax processes and workflows are being created. It's not busy yet. All CPA offices get busy in March and April. Even the ones like us that have workflows, systems, and processes in place. There are more clients asking questions and coming into the office. We have more meetings that are booked. December and January are good months to make a switch for the upcoming season. I also see a lot of clients that make a switch right after tax season. Maybe they were with a CPA for a long time, their level of service has consistently gone down, and they have a really bad experience with the tax season. They're like, "Nope, I'm done. I'm going." So, I would say just try to avoid switching around April 15th or April 12th, right before the deadline.

Outside of that, work with your new CPA and see what they feel is the best solution for you and what your business has and needs. After that, get all of your prior year data. Most CPAs do things through a secure portal. Make sure that you have one. If you have QuickBooks online, it's really important to make sure that you're the master administrator of your QuickBooks online. If not, you need to get that done ASAP. If your current CPA is the master admin, you need to have them switch that to you. A little disclaimer is to never, ever let anybody else have the master admin rights of your QuickBooks, because that means that they legally have ownership of your ledger. You always need to have that. That is yours. It's your ledger. You need to have it. If your CPA currently pays for it, you need to take that off of them.

You need to pay for your own ledger so that it's yours forever and ever. If and when you get audited by the IRS, they may want access to your QuickBooks. It's really important that you have it.

These are the things you need. Make sure you have master admin rights to your QuickBooks. Make sure you have all of your prior year tax returns, and any deliverables that they've given you. Make sure you have copies of those. If for some reason you don't, request and get those copies so you have everything that you need and securely put them on your server or in your records—even outside of the portal. Most CPAs, if a client no longer needs service from us, they still have access to our portal. But just in case, make sure you have access to copies of all your records.

After that, you can disengage with your current CPA. Sometimes clients say, am I required to do that? You're not required to, but it is good professional etiquette to do so. If you've been with your CPA, he has you on his tax list and probably has it allocated so that he can help accommodate you in the upcoming tax season. It's just good practice. Even a quick email will suffice to say, "Hey, I've really enjoyed working with you. I'm going to go in a different direction moving forward, and I'm no longer going to need your services." It's just etiquette. It's kind, it's respectful. Sometimes A CPA might say, "Hey, I really appreciate if there's any feedback you could give me." That's a great opportunity to give them some feedback in a kind and respectful way that may actually help them build their practice and be a better business owner.

In that disengagement letter you might say, "I give you my permission to talk with my new CPA, if there are any questions or anything like that." A lot of times, if you have your complete set of records, the new CPA does not have to work with the old CPA on anything. But I've had cases where there's a depreciation schedule, and there's something that's missing that just didn't get put in that client's copy of their tax return. However, I'm not allowed to reach out to the old CPA. I need the client's permission. So, make sure that with the information, you give permission to communicate between the old CPA and the new CPA. It's helpful in case there is anything that needs to be discussed after that. Make the switch with confidence.

By now, you've extended the olive branch, you fired your CPA, and you've engaged with a new CPA. You and your new CPA have planned out how and when you're going to implement the switch and onboarding of all your new services. You made sure that you have all of your prior year data. You gave a kind and respectful disengagement letter to your current CPA. You gave permission for your new and your old CPA to communicate, if necessary. That gives you what you need to switch confidently to your new CPA. We are also going to put a disengagement letter template in the conclusion of this book. With these processes, you can confidently make the switch.

CHAPTER 17

Maximizing Your Financial Potential

I'm really excited to dive into this chapter because it's popular right now on social media. Different platforms and people are digging into loopholes based around maximizing your financial potential with investments and real estate planning. Specifically for my clients that are real estate investors, they often do it on the side. This is really popular right now.

A good, licensed CPA, does tax planning, is proactive, and does everything we've covered. You've fired your CPA, you found your new CPA, and then in the last chapter, we went through how to actually make the switch. From there, we look at specifics.

I get snapshots of texts and emails and advice given online that is so incorrect and so wrong.

There's a lot of bad advice that gets misconstrued from experts online. Do you remember that game Telephone we played when we were little? You sat in a circle, and you started with a word or phrase and Bobby Joe told Susie-Q the secret, and then it went around the circle and, at the very end, the last person said what it was.

It got so misconstrued, and it was always really funny. I've actually done that in a mastermind just to show the power of how communication can be misconstrued, but this happens a lot in the realms of tax planning and financial advice. Billy Bob tells you something that his cousin's CPA did, then you tell somebody else that has a completely different setup so that isn't applicable to them, but they take it, and they add their two cents on it, and then it goes down the line. It's completely falsified and misconstrued by the time it gets to you.

What are we going to do? You're going to roll your eyes because I've said this in every chapter. You're always going to make sure that you work with a licensed CPA who is also a strategic CPA who does tax planning and will go down this road with you. Hopefully, this is the one you interviewed and used our checklist with, and now you're on board with them. Make sure they're your one-stop-shop for tax planning, for financial advice, financial planning, and whatever you need.

For real estate investment, the number one thing I can recommend is to make sure you're getting the most bang for your tax buck. Don't roll your eyes just because this isn't fun, and it's not sexy; it's required. Your books need to be clean. You need to have job costing, and know the per property or per project income, revenue, and any gains on sales of each property. You need all of your improvements, all of your expenses. If you do not have that, I guarantee you're overpaying in tax, and that doesn't have anything to do with tax planning. You have to have your bookkeeping done. The second thing for your CPA really depends on how your CPA works. I personally do not ask for receipts. I only ask for receipts if it seems like something I need to dig into to actually make sure it's substantiated. The IRS says the burden of proof is on the taxpayer in an audit.

That means that I'm creating these tax returns from your records based off what you tell me. You need to keep your receipts, okay? You need a receipt for every purchase you have for any project, any expense, any improvements to be able to substantiate and prove to the IRS that it's an accurate business deduction for tax purposes. Now, there are a lot of different things that you can do. You can do something as simple as having a manila folder for each project. You can keep it digitized and have Receipt Bank or another app where you can just snap pictures and have them based in the cloud and at that point, once they're there, they're never going to fade.

You can organize by year and by project and at that point, you can actually throw your hard copies away if they're in the electronic version. Okay? The third thing you need to understand is depreciation and how it affects your real estate projects and how it works. I will not specifically go into what you can do, because those rules change every single year, and I don't know when you're actually reading this book or what edition of this book it is.

Your licensed CPA, your strategic partner who does tax planning, will know those rules and that's something that's going to come into play every single year, especially as you plan and grow. It could be that you're in real estate, your goal is to amass 20 residential properties to have a cash flow of X to be able to retire at X. How do depreciation rules help offset taxable income in different years? This will be really pivotal when you buy some of those properties and or when you do improvements or upgrades to those properties. In some years, you're going to get a bigger bang for your tax bucks than other cost segregation studies.

This is something that's getting more popular. A cost segregation study is when you go to a licensed engineering firm, and they do a formal study that they give to you on your property.

It's an investment property that you have. A residential property, for example, you have to typically depreciate over 27 1/2 years. If it's a commercial property, you are required to depreciate that over 39 years. Let's talk about a commercial property, because sometimes the cost of a cost segregation study is that you usually get a much bigger bang for your buck when you're talking about a larger commercial property. Let's say that you buy a million-dollar property—and that's just the property—you don't get to depreciate land.

Let's say that the value of the property that you bought is a million dollars. So, under normal depreciation, you have to depreciate that over 39 years, which means you get to write off essentially $25,641 a year over 39 years.

A cost segregation study looks at that $1 million property and says, of this $1 million property X percentage is actually 39 years of life. It's the actual building, the nuts and bolts, the big stuff, the HVAC and electrical and equipment systems. That's 30% of it. That has a seven-year life, so 30% of our purchase price can cost segregate and allocate that out over a smaller useful life. This means you get more bang for your tax buck upfront. Again, it's not that you're getting extra depreciation—it means that you get to take a bigger chunk on any component of that depreciable asset in a useful life that's more appropriate. But it means that it might be depreciated over seven years or 15 years instead of the 39 years, and you get much bigger bang for your tax buck upfront instead of over 39 years.

This is very powerful, especially if you have a property that is a high net-worth residential property or a commercial property. There are a ton of different companies that you can work with. I always recommend you go with one that has licensed engineers. If you get audited, the IRS will want to look at your cost segregation study, so you want to make sure that you are going with a good company. Another one for real estate to think about is a 1031 exchange. A little word on 1031 exchanges: they are very highly regulated and audited by the IRS. I always recommend going with a CPA who specializes in 1031s. Because I do a lot of broad tax planning, I actually refer this out to a real estate attorney because I've had a couple of brand new tax clients who switch over to Sarah Jones CPA, and they turn all their stuff into me and they say, "Oh, by the way, we did this and I want to do a 1031 on this one, and I say, Oh, buddy, you're going to be so upset, but this is not how it works, and a 1031 is very specific."

You have to turn in and allocate and designate the days that you're going to do this by. Otherwise, the IRS says you can't do it, so it's very specific. Essentially what you're able to do in a 1031 is, whatever your taxable gain would've been in an investment property, you're able to completely defer that into your new property. If you invest into a new property, which is a great opportunity—especially if your goal is to amass and do this over and over—you really can get some strategy to continuously defer those gains.

The most common mistake specific to real estate is following advice online, which we've talked about. We're no longer going to do that because you've now read *Fire My CPA*. Now, you are working with a licensed CPA who does tax planning and is proactive, so you're going to stop following nonsense online. I see some wonky stuff just from people following other people online that say some really crazy things.

The second major issue I see with real estate investment is not working with the CPA. Again, this doesn't apply to you now because you've read *Fire My CPA*. You already fired your old CPA. You're working now with a great, proactive, synergistic, part-of-your-team CPA who is going to give you a roadmap for success, both and long-term.

I don't want to go into the specifics of real estate tax law, because it changes every single year. There are some loopholes and things you can do some years and then other years you can't do. I don't know when you're reading this book, and I don't know what edition you have of this book, but what I will say is that real estate has a ton of opportunities. In fact, a lot of my clients that are business owners will start out with success in their business and they'll begin to diversify their income streams by investing in real estate.

They do this to get rental income for long-term capital appreciation of the property and those revenue streams, but also because there are some tax benefits. You need to work with a CPA who does tax planning, who knows real estate tax law, and can help guide you through this as you buy each property and as you grow. Make sure that your long-term goals really align with the tax planning that you can put into place.

CHAPTER 18

The CPA as a Pillar in Risk Management and Asset Protection

Time to move forward? That new CPA you have should be a pillar to you, your company, and your family, as well as your wealth building, risk management, and asset protection. Okay?

We're going to go over some strategies and good advice to have a comprehensive risk management and wealth preservation plan that is all encompassing. This comes after you have gone through all the other steps. Let's talk about risk management—your risk and asset protection. Now, I'll tell you, I'm a CPA. I am not an attorney.

It's not okay for a CPA under AICPA, who governs CPAs in all 50 states, to practice law. So, as a CPA, what can I not do? I cannot set up an entity for you. I cannot practice law. I can advise. I can give you tax strategy and tax advice on such issues, but as a CPA, I cannot do legal work. A good CPA will always partner with a great attorney group that works hand in hand for tax planning and estate planning. For example, Sarah Jones CPA works really closely with an attorney group that are board certified estate planners and business attorneys. If we have a tax plan or an estate plan that we're putting together for asset protection or for tax strategies, I do the tax and the implementation. They do all of the legal work inherent to that process.

That's really important. If you have a CPA who's doing legal work, you need not to use that CPA, because they are doing something that is not okay, as per the AICPA who governs licensed CPAs.

So, let's dive into it. Risk management in asset protection is going to be a little bit different for each individual. Let's say you have a January health resolution, and you go to a personal trainer, your plan is going to be completely different or at least a little different. It's going to be custom to you. My plan might be different than your plan because everybody's different. Everybody has unique situations, unique goals, and your plan should be according to your unique needs and set of goals. Okay? So, get your new CPA involved in this process. Make sure the CPA who you work with is ready for a conversation about asset and liability protection, about risk management, and get an attorney group involved for your benefit for both short and long-term.

That's a recurring theme here. We don't want what's best for you right now. We want what's best for you right now, down the road, and way down the road. We want you to be successful at all times.

Asset protection is custom-based. This looks a little bit similar to how the process looks for tax planning. You typically turn in all of the information that you have—all of your prior tax returns, if you have any type of entity set up or any structure, any diagrams of stuff that you have, any formal tax memorandums from anything you had done. All of that stuff needs to come to your CPA, and you do also need to give that CPA permission to talk to the attorney about your situation. It is so specific and custom-based it will need to be looked at on an individual case basis, according to what your goals are.

Your CPA will do a review, just like at the beginning of tax planning, going through and looking at it and seeing the strengths of your setup, and then also the disadvantages or risks inherent in how you're set up. After that, they will get with that attorney for their input, before approaching you with, "Hey, this is what we found. This is what's really good. This is not good. Here's actually an opportunity for asset and liability protection."

A lot of times, through that process, you're looking at it for asset and liability protection, but sometimes you also find opportunities for tax planning inherent in the process. From there, you'll engage to get the asset and the liability protection done, or the estate planning done, per se.

Sometimes that happens as well, and again, you need a licensed attorney to practice law. A CPA cannot practice law. Any setups, any restructuring, anything like that must be done by a licensed attorney that has experience. If those documents are not accurate, if they are not done properly, you actually could be exposing yourself to additional risk. If there are cracks or something is falling through, you are in a worse situation than you were without any of this setup before.

After that, typically we're going to do a revised tax memorandum or a formal memorandum. The attorneys typically do one on their side for all the legal work. Your CPA will then go back, do an updated tax memorandum, including your new setup to use each entity. They'll include what the purpose is, what the benefits and all of that are, so that you have a tangible reference guide for your success and how to use this.

Again, if you have a question, sometimes that question is at midnight and you cannot get your CPA on the phone, so that's your reference guide. What I will say for legal needs—anytime you are looking to get asset liability protection done or you're wanting to look at estate planning, you need to go through a very similar process as when you are looking for a CPA. Use that checklist. You're going to want to do the same process for an attorney. Now, a good CPA like Sarah Jones CPA, is strategic. We work very closely with an attorney group already. So, since you have fired your CPA and gone through the process and you have a new CPA who is a strategic partner with your business, they most likely have an attorney.

That is absolutely where you should go first, because they already have a good working relationship. They're going to glue everything together when there are questions that come up. But if for some reason, they do not work with an attorney already, search for an estate planning attorney or a business attorney. I always like to do an estate planning attorney because as you grow, they're going to have a good mindset for succession planning, wealth preservation, and generational wealth. Look at the reviews. Interview a couple, two or three, like we did in the CPA checklist. Tell them about yourself. Tell them your goals, your values, your mission, and what you want to accomplish. Take your tax returns. If you have any structure, set up a diagram of that. Share with them everything that you have.

Have them do a review for you. Put together a proposal for asset and liability protection along the way. There also might be some tax strategies and opportunities that arise. Go through that with them. Then you will engage with them and get that process done. They will implement the plan, put it into place, and then give you those formal memorandums, and then you can give that to your CPA. They can integrate that for you, keep you compliant, and have you on your way to make sure that you are the most strategic for tax, but you get that asset and liability protection that you need. Once you're aligned with an attorney and a CPA who will be there for you both now and in the future, you're on a road to success.

CHAPTER 19

Communication is Key - Building a Relationship with Your CPA

Now we come to one of the most important chapters, concept-wise. This is imperative to focus on with your CPA, and actually it's the key to everything in life. We are talking about communication and cultivating the relationship for future growth in building a relationship with your CPA. So, these are techniques and tips on how to establish and maintain effective communication.

I have read books about communication. I could write a whole book just about communication with your CPA, because it's in every single relationship. If you want to bring down a country, what do you do? They say to attack communication. How does a marriage fall down? They don't communicate. How do partnerships collapse? The same way. I'm always the CPA who might be brought in from an attorney group on a partnership gone bad. It's usually because they didn't communicate.

Communication is so pivotal to everything that I just said. Communication is always behind any thriving organization, whether it be a country, a city, a county, a family, a marriage, a business, or a partnership. Communication is so vital in everything that we do. I would guess without knowing your specific situation with your prior CPA, you had a breakdown in communication, because when you saw the book title *Fire My CPA*, it resonated with you. It was that gut punch and you're like, "Oh, I need this book. This speaks to me." That means that you did not have a good communication channel or a good communication relationship with your CPA for whatever reason. So, let's talk about it. Remember earlier, we had that checklist for an interview with a CPA who we talked about?

You should have been able to pull that from the back of the book when you went on those interviews with CPAs. What did we do? We were looking at your communication needs and how you are wired and what your expectations were. Remember, before we even talked about what we needed from a CPA or what that ideal relationship was, we looked at you first, and I feel like we need to do that here as well.

How do you communicate? For example, do you like a phone call? Do you like to meet in person? Do you like an email? Do you like a text? If you want to communicate with me, you send me an email. If you text me, you will not get a response, because I do not have my phone with me during the workday.

If you call, text, and email me at the exact same time, everybody who knows me knows I will respond to your email, because that's my workflow. That's how I work, and that's how I communicate. Because I'm a CPA, and I like everything in writing, I like an audit trail to remember exactly what we talked about. Email is my jam.

So, what is your jam? What do you like to do and how do you communicate? Because it's really important that you share that with your CPA. We went through that in that checklist—figuring out your communication styles, your needs, your mission, your values, your short-term and long-term goals, and then creating your ideal situation with a CPA. And then, you went through and actually shared that with the CPA you chose to work with.

So, by the time you're on this chapter, maybe you've interviewed those CPAs and have your new CPA, and I want to make sure that your communication stays strong so that you guys can have a mutually successful relationship, both short-term and long-term. Like we talked about, there's a ton of synergy built through staying with your CPA for a long time.

Let's say that your preferred communication channel is email. You need to make sure that you have relayed that to your CPA, which you should have already done if you went through the process and used the checklist.

Let's say, during tax season, they're missing some documents from you. In their process, their administrative assistant or their office manager goes through everything, and they call clients to tell them that things are missing and it's holding up the tax process. They know that you prefer to have email communication. It might be insightful for them to really know that and note that on your account so that when she's going through and making those calls, she can send you an email instead, because you've specified, "Hey, this is kind of how I like to be communicated with by a CPA firm."

When new clients come to us, we always ask how they heard about us or how they were referred, because we like to track that. Sometimes it's a brand-new client who are new business owners, or they've just gotten to the point where they're finding a CPA, but a lot of times they were with a prior CPA, and I always like to ask how their experience was.

Every time, they say, "I never hear from my CPA. I'll send an email and it takes them three weeks to respond. Or, when I do hear from my CPA, they have absolutely no idea what they're talking about." Both of those issues are communication issues. They're probably a great technical CPA, but they're not that strategic partner that you're wanting.

In a CPA firm, it's all about the systems and processes of how their team works. You are most likely a business owner reading this book, so you have systems and processes and deliverables to your clients in some shape or form. You understand this as well. As you grow, you have more demands, and those demands require you to change and pivot, to put the systems and processes in place to make sure you can accommodate the needs of the additional clients that you have, that you want, and you need. You want to serve, but you need to do it in a way that your level of service doesn't decrease.

So, communication of systems and processes in a CPA firm is absolutely key to your success with your CPA. You want a CPA who's already forward thinking. Maybe you're going to a CPA who's smaller. Maybe they're boutique. There is nothing wrong with that in any way, shape, or form. In fact, you usually get a little bit more service with a smaller boutique firm, but that smaller boutique firm is ultimately going to grow over time. You want to make sure that they're already thinking about that, so they don't turn into the big, huge, unfriendly, turnover firm. You want them to keep that touchpoint of a small firm.

If they've got systems and processes on their mind, that is less likely to happen. I have a master's degree in accounting. They do not teach us in school how to have a CPA firm. They really don't. You are taught how to be compliant, how to do things accurately and technically be an accountant. How you learn that is through business ownership. And how I learned it is through a lot of mistakes, and trial and error. When I went out on my own in May of 2018, I went through a lot of mistakes. Sometimes those mistakes were embarrassing, and sometimes they were good learning experiences, but that's how you learn.

As a client, you might say, "I want my CPA's cell phone number and I can just call them, and they answer." You really don't want that. If you're getting a CPA who answers every time you call, that probably means that they're very, very early in their journey. There is nothing wrong with that, but they're going to grow. I'm saying this because I absolutely went through the same thing. When I first started out, everybody had my cell phone number. I was on access, and you do that because you're learning and you want to serve, and I wanted to help everybody. But I learned very quickly that if I'm not the best Sarah, and if I'm not taking care of myself, and if I'm not there for my family, and if I'm not present as a mother and as a wife, I'm not going to be a good CPA for everybody.

There should be checks and balances and healthy boundaries to make sure that I can fulfill all of my God-given duties and talents and responsibilities. That comes with actually being able to put my phone away and time block. So, if you have a CPA who does that, I would caution you that's not going to last long. Typically, when a CPA says yes to everybody, that's when things start falling through the cracks.

If you call the number on Google and the CPA answers the phone, that's probably a sign that they're really new, and they don't have those systems and processes in place. It also means they do everything.

They're going to say yes to everything, but they're going to have a really hard time at actually executing that. What you want is a CPA who has a team, an administrative assistant, somebody that does things. You should have to book a consult with a CPA, and at first glance, it might be, "Oh, that's kind of stuffy. I don't like that." I'm telling you; I've done this long enough to know you want a CPA who has systems and processes in place, just like your doctor. They have systems and processes in place so that the doctor can give utmost care and service and respect and be present to every single patient that comes in.

It's the same thing here. You want a CPA who has a team and has those systems and processes in place. Now, the only caveat that I say to that is everything has a time and a place to make sure that it all gets handled. Now, if your CPA is doing your bookkeeping and payroll, if there is ever an emergency that arises, they should have a contingency. What is an accounting emergency? Let's say that you get a letter from the IRS saying that they're going to seize your assets. That is an emergency. Or if your CPA is doing your payroll and one of your employees didn't get paid, that is an emergency. Your CPA should have contingency plans in place when things like that happen and need to be addressed immediately.

And if a CPA has good systems and processes in place, they will have contingency plans and can help you immediately if needed.

What's the biggest takeaway? Know your communication style and match it with a CPA. Again, if you went through chapter nine, and did the checklist and interviewed CPAs, you've already done this, but this is really just a reminder that now you have your badass CPA that you have found through this process. Make sure you're always having a mutually successful relationship, both now and in the future with your CPA.

So, how often should you be communicating? I'll tell you how we do this at Sarah Jones CPA. No matter what kind of client you are, we have a weekly newsletter email that goes out to everybody. It puts you at the forefront of any new tax legislation, giving you a good pulse. We do a monthly video for all of our clients going over current trends and things to remember. It's generic, but it's the stuff that you just need to remember and keep at the forefront of your mind.

Our clients hear from us weekly. It's not anything specific. I'm not reaching out to our thousands of clients, but it's something, a pulse from our office, to keep you in the loop. That right there is a good sign of a good CPA.

You want to make sure that you look at exactly what is specified for the level of service that you're wanting and needing. Commonly in bookkeeping, you're going to have reports every single month on the 15th, and a lot of times it comes with a meeting once a month, and it's up to you to click on that calendar link to book the meeting. Sometimes, in the engagement letter, it might be specified, and it's already built in, but monthly is a great pulse. If we're doing CFO work for you, Sarah Jones CPA has accountability meetings once a month. If you're an investment client of ours, typically, again, you're going to be on those pulses of where you're going to have a newsletter weekly. You're going to get a video monthly, just with current trends and topics.

Usually with our investment clients, we have a quarterly check-in and then a tax planning meeting once a year, but those can be custom built. What I'm really getting at is to make sure whatever your engagement level is with your CPA, it should specify the communication terms to keep you guys in a mutually successful relationship all year long. That's really important. If you're just a tax client, let's say that you have a smaller business, or a bookkeeping team that's internal, and your CPA is only doing your taxes, I still like a quarterly check-in.

I think that it's far enough apart that there's always going to be something new that's going on that you can talk about, but it's close enough together that it allows us to be proactive and talk so that nothing falls through the cracks. What I don't like is when I have a tax client and I talk to them just during tax season, and I don't hear from them all year. I don't feel like it's good for either of us. It's not strategic or proactive, but that should give you a good pulse. What I would like to say more than anything is that communication, by far, is one of the most important things with your CPA. Make sure that you find a good CPA who will have those systems and processes in place and make communication the forefront of your relationship. Because what we all want here is for you to be with your CPA for many years and have a really successful, huge return on your investment. So, do what you need to do, and have a strategic partner that communicates regularly.

The CPA for Generational Wealth - Beyond Your Lifetime

Chapter 20 is all about the CPA for generational wealth beyond your lifetime. Basically, we're planning for your future with your CPA's guidance on wealth transfer. It's how to work with the CPA throughout your life because that's what you want. Just like having a doctor that you really care about and knows your medical history, you want to use that doctor for your health throughout your lifetime, even when your health is different. You have different needs and wants and different things for the doctor to help with. And then of course, when you grow your family, you have children and grandchildren, you want to continue. This should be the same thing with your CPA.

As a review for what you need: your CPA should be a one-stop shop. Make sure they do your wealth planning. Make sure that they do your insurance planning. Make sure that they have good ties with an attorney. Make sure they do tax planning. Make sure that they are a heck of a CPA. Like we covered in chapter nine, you fired your old CPA, interviewed 3-5 new CPAs, used the checklist in our resources, and you've signed with a new CPA.

This chapter is really just to piggyback on the last chapter, which was all about communication with your CPA. This is what your roadmap to success looks like with the CPA firm. We're going to see an example of when you're first starting and how to continue all through your life. Again, a CPA is a long-term relationship.

Your CPA should grow and evolve and succeed along with you in your life. You don't want to listen to a 70-year-old CPA who does manual work and is not up with the times. That is not the CPA we're looking for, and I guarantee that that's not the CPA who you picked. If you went through the process and the checklist and interviews earlier, your CPA should work with you, with your kids, with your partners, with your legal team—everything all in one.

Let's say that you are a business owner, and it's your first year of business. Your CPA comes alongside you and does your tax return at the very beginning, okay? You don't even need bookkeeping at this point. You just started your business. They keep you compliant for tax. Then, the next year you actually start growing. You have clients, you have employees. This CPA should now do your bookkeeping and your payroll. This means they do all your categorizing. They give you monthly reports. You might be having a monthly meeting to go over operations. They're processing your payroll.

They keep you super, super up to date. You've got all that information to make real time decisions in your business. It's always clean. If you need information to make decisions in your business, you've got it. Most importantly, when it comes to tax time, all of the information is done. The hard part is done. They take that information and prepare your tax return with it.

Let's say you progress a couple years down the road, and you've hit seven figures. You've got a bigger team now, bigger operations, and you're really ready to scale at this point. You should. Absolutely, you need some tax planning, but your CPA should already be alongside you. They're seeing those books; they're seeing that tax return every year. They should prompt that conversation and tax planning should get done, but also, when you hit seven figures, you should also—in addition to a great bookkeeping team that your CPA is doing for you—have CFO coaching.

You say, "I have this business that I've built it from the ground up. I'm now at seven figures. I have goals to do mid-seven figures. I want to do this. I have these goals and I want to exit at some point and sell this bad boy."

A CFO coaching engagement will take your specific goals and give you a roadmap to success, a custom-based dashboard, monitor your cash flow in your specific goals, and give you tangible action items every single month for you and for your team to actually achieve those goals. This is super, super powerful, okay? At that point, you've got CFO coaching, and you're really ramping up operations. You're achieving those income goals. You have tax planning in place, so you feel confident in your tax bill. You understand that you pay taxes as you earn more, but you're doing it in the most efficient way possible, and you feel confident and comfortable with the plan that you have with your CPA at this point.

When you start to achieve some of those growth goals, it's time to look at some asset protection planning and also some estate planning, and that's a conversation that your CPA should spur and bring in licensed attorneys to help with. They know what to do because they've been with you since you were a baby business. This is almost their baby too. They feel like they're vested in your success, and as you grow, they bring in these additional pieces to make sure that you are handled properly. Let's say that now you've grown to a point where you're doing so much, you've got all that asset protection in place. You have some more time on your hands, so now you meet the girl of your dreams, you get married, you have kids. At this point, a CPA should come alongside you and make sure you understand the tax implications of that.

What are some of the credits that you get? What can you do to set these children up for success? What do we need to do? Do we need life insurance? Your CPA should go down that journey with you as you go through these milestones in life. If your CPA does your wealth management, which I really highly recommend that they do, they can help you set up and manage college funds. They set up retirement plans, and a lot of times that is part of the tax planning process as well because those are mostly tax advantage plans.

We've got tax planning, CFO coaching, and now you have your asset and estate plan, insurance, and investments. You got married, you have kids. Those kids are in college. Now, let's say that you're tired, and you're ready to retire. You've loved it, but your company is a well-oiled machine, and you want to sell this bad boy. A CPA and your attorney will be part of that succession planning. Additionally, make sure that before you go into that, you have everything you need to go through due diligence, which is a breeze if you've worked with a CPA, because that's all under a CPA's scope to do. If and when you exit, we do it in the most tax efficient manner possible, and we plan for it with a great succession plan from that point. In retirement, having a CPA help you as you take pension or retirement funds out is done in the most effective way possible.

If you're working with a CPA who's managing your retirement planning and your wealth planning as well, it's one and done. You guys have those conversations very easily, and you're not having to go to a CPA as well as a financial advisor and having to get them done again. Get a CPA who's strategic and does everything in one. You have all of your asset and estate planning done, and you can rest easy in that. And, when the time comes, they can step in because you have the proper planning done, and you avoid probate. Everything's done in the most efficient tax way possible, and your family, of course, is grieving you, but they are comforted in the fact that you have set everything up properly.

You have peace of mind when all of your affairs are in order. They're done in the most efficient way possible, and you worked really hard to keep more of your tax and more of your wealth to give to your family instead of overpaying it to the IRS. All of this is possible because you had proper planning done years and years and years ago. You've been with that same strategic CPA who has gone down this journey with you through different life events. So that, my friend, is what you want with your CPA. Again, the whole point of *Fire My CPA* is not to rag on CPAs. I am a CPA. But I want to make sure you are getting what you need out of your CPA, that you have that partner who truly is an extension of your team, someone who helps you now, all the way until the very end of your career, and then when it's time, the end of your life. You want a trusted advisor and friend who handles all of your financial affairs for you and your family.

CHAPTER 21

Your Next Steps

You've done it. You've made it to the end of *Fire My CPA*. At last, you've reached that resource chapter that we've talked about throughout the book. These are the tools and solutions you can put into play to make sure that you are able to fire your CPA, get the CPA you need, and have the resources you need as well.

So, if you're reading this chapter, or if you're one of those people who go to the very end of the book because you want the goods without reading it, I appreciate your efficiency. Bare minimum, you need to go through Chapter 15. Chapter 15 tells you how to disengage with your current CPA and explains why we have the checklist in this chapter. You can then use it in interviews and find a good CPA, because that process is key to your long-term success.

I don't want you to have to come back to this book next year if the one that you chose isn't a great fit. You have to go through the steps. This book is a comprehensive tool. You should actually bring those steps in Chapter 15 with you to that interview process with a potential CPA. In that chapter, we talked about soul searching and figuring out how you operate and what you want.

I think that's really important to share and acknowledge.

Recognize who you are and what you need, then share that with the CPA in the interview process, just to make sure that you guys are a great fit. Okay?

You're going to find a really simple template you can use to disengage with your prior CPA, and also a template you can use to engage with a new CPA. Once you find one you like, you can disengage with your current CPA in a very respectful and kind manner, giving them a heads up before you engage with the new CPA. I'm also putting a communication summary in here as to what you should expect, or what I feel like are good guidelines for communication based on different levels of service. For example, if you just have a tax accountant, how should you communicate with that tax accountant to be strategic? How do you communicate the need for tax planning if you only have bookkeeping or only have a CFO?

So, I added that summary of communication. If you remember, we had an entire chapter on communication and how important that was, and I really feel like, even if you have a badass CPA, if you never communicate with them, you're really missing a huge opportunity. Communication is key.

From everybody here at Sarah Jones CPA, thanks so much for going on this journey with us. Use these tools. We really appreciate you, and I would love to hear from you. Please feel free to reach out, and we'll chat soon.

About Sarah Jones CPA

All right, so this whole entire book, you've been with me, Sarah Jones. I'm super passionate about educating people about what CPAs are, what you should do, what you shouldn't do, what you should be looking for, and really just taking control of your financial health. But for those people that read this book and want to fire their CPA, I wanted to let you know how to work with Sarah Jones CPA. We are a great CPA firm, and my wealth of knowledge and everything that I've shared with you, I've integrated into my firm. This is how we operate. We operate this way because I have been in the industry for over 15 years, and I've learned what to do and what not to do when creating a CPA firm.

So, in saying that, this little bonus section here is all about my firm, who we are, what we do, and what you can get by working with us. I'm the owner of Sarah Jones CPA. Again, I quit my full-time job in May of 2018, and I'm so glad that I did. I really enjoy serving our clients, and we make a great impact for them. We are a licensed CPA firm in the state of Texas. I say that I'm in Houston because, unless you're in the local area, you don't know where we are—about an hour north of Houston.

I'm from a tiny town called Willis, Texas, and our office is right on the cusp of Willis and Conroe, Texas. We serve the local community, but I also am an enrolled agent. I'm licensed by the IRS in all 50 states, and we do have quite a few clients out of state as well.

I started this firm in May of 2018. I have a master's degree in business administration and finance. I also have a master's degree in accounting and another master's degree in finance. I have a Certificate in Financial Management from Cornell University and I'm also a certified tax planner and a certified CFO.

I have been married to my husband for almost 13 years. We have four children, three grown girls, and we have a spunky, 9-year-old. We are members of Under Over Fellowship. We enjoy traveling, working out, and spending time with family. A huge part of my time is spent around our CPA firm, because I'm very passionate about it. When I started, it was just me. We now have a team of 11.

If you want to find out about us, you can go to our website, sarahjonescpa.com. Our mission statement as to why we exist and why we do what we do is *Build, Protect, and Grow.* We help our clients build their dreams, protect their assets, and grow their legacy. Our belief is that we do simple reports and strategic tax solutions. We love accounting tax and tax planning, but we understand that most of our clients don't. We want the easiest, simplest means to an end to know their accounting and tax return is accurate and complete for our monthly clients. We won't send you 50 pages of reports, because we know that these are going to end up in the trash can. We will send you a simple, easy to read report that will give you clarity on your business.

We find that simple reports are the best way to give actionable steps and items that you can integrate into your business each month. Strategic tax solutions to tax planning are the foundation for long-term success often overlooked by many clients that come to Sarah Jones CPA. We are extremely passionate about tax savings. Every tax return is processed by our internal team, reviewed, and approved by Sarah Jones, CPA. All of our tax planning clients work directly with me, Sarah Jones. Again, we strongly feel that we are called to be different. Our tax planning is an area where we really shine and are set apart from other CPA firms. So, what do we do here at Sarah Jones CPA? What are the different services that we offer?

We offer accounting and bookkeeping. Are you wanting clarity in your business, needing improved efficiencies, and looking for solid reporting on income and expense trends on a monthly basis?

Sarah Jones CPA can provide monthly services custom built for your needs. We offer simple bookkeeping all the way up to full CFO services. Our professional staff has full cycle experience and a wide range of industry expertise to provide the customized service you need to achieve your financial goals. Our services range from simple QuickBooks online management and monthly bookkeeping, with basic financial reports on a monthly basis, to complete job costing engagements for teams that really need insight to propel their business.

Bottom line, our team can get the job done. You can trust Sarah Jones CPA to provide quality and timely insight into your business. Our services are custom built per client with services ranging from full cycle bookkeeping, cash or accrual basis accounting needs, cash flow design and management with team meetings and reporting budget design goal and management, KPI and financial dashboards for investors and board of directors or stakeholders, internal management and cost reporting, bank reconciliation and balance sheet reconciliations, accounts receivable and accounts payable, design management and strategy, preparing financial statements, payroll processing including 1099s and W2s, internal team training for onsite, daily oversight, accounting, consultation design, or implementation oversight.

We do full-service tax. Tax preparation is not as simple as it once was with tax laws changing every year and the added complexity of COVID-19. The tax team at Sarah Jones CPA has you covered. A knowledgeable, competent CPA is a valuable asset to your family and is often a huge return on your investment, not only in the tax years, but for many years to come. We stay abreast of the tax laws each year and make sure to review your situations for tax deductions and credits. Again, these change every year. Making sure your CPA team goes the extra mile is important. The team at Sarah Jones CPA have tax organizers in place to capture any and all potential tax opportunities, and each client is given the utmost care and attention. Our office operates on a tax portal. Clients have the option to complete the entire tax process virtually.

With the help of our team, we also have our tax organizer folders ready to go in our office. For clients who prefer an in-person meeting experience, all tax returns are personally reviewed by me, Sarah Jones, CPA. Each client reviews all work before anything is filed, and all returns are e-filed with the IRS for quick processing. We provide estimated tax forms for the upcoming year and send out tax reminders to our clients throughout the year. We enjoy communicating with our clients all year long, not just in April. Additionally, clients have the opportunity to have a consultation directly with me or one of our tax managers through the year as needed for our business clients. We have a close advisory relationship with our business owners. We send out frequent tax reminders, our tax tips newsletter, and we are active on social media platforms for our clients. We advocate for education, knowledge, and strategy.

Owning your own business is a job in itself. We can handle the tax aspect for you. Tax laws change frequently, and our team stays abreast of these changes for you. Our tax team is led by me, Sarah

Jones, CPA, who oversees all of the work. You won't be a number here at Sarah Jones CPA. You are family. We handle all types of business structure returns and keep up with the different due dates and the different state requirements. We also work closely with our business owners to ensure they're strategic in their setup operations and advise on how to strategically pay less tax.

In our tax planning, we feel that this is actually the foundation of everything that you do as a business owner. It's one of the most solid investments you can make for your future and your family, as well as for your business. Sometimes, tax planning can literally be the difference of hundreds of thousands of dollars paid in tax over your life. Our tax planning services are what set Sarah Jones CPA apart from most other firms. We enjoy working closely with our clients and communicating with them throughout the year.

December 31st is too late for tax planning. We take a much more proactive approach. All clients have access to our calendars and can book consultations as frequently as they choose for both our individual tax clients and our business owners. Tax planning starts with a complimentary consultation with Sarah Jones, CPA, either virtually or in our Conroe office. A review of prior year tax returns and current year financials is done and Sarah Jones custom builds tax plans per client. Typically, our business owners save an average of 20% to 30% on taxes with proper planning.

Our CFO services are for those clients who already have a CPA and bookkeeping, and most likely it's being done by Sarah Jones CPA, and you have hit that seven-figure mark. You want laser focus and clarity on how to take your business to the next level. You need custom built dashboards with goals and KPIs for your team. You need to increase your cash flow and you want actionable items that you can integrate on a monthly basis to actually achieve your goals. So, CFO coaching is something that I recently got certified in and we're rolling it out for 2024. You can do a complimentary consultation with me about what your goals are and see how we could do that together and I would custom build a CFO engagement for you.

Another new service we rolled out is wealth advisory services. Phil Jones is a licensed stockbroker and has been in the industry for over 20 years. He's the leader of our team here, and Phil's knowledge coupled with my tax expertise creates a team that does full wealth management services and advisory services, and also insurance services for those needs you have for life insurance to cover your family. There is actually some tax strategy involved with some of those outside of the box insurance planning tools that we may recommend to a client to diversify their holdings.

All of our team has the passion to educate, give clarity, and bring forth empowerment. Ultimately, at Sarah Jones CPA, we want to help you get rid of that fear-based mentality.

That's something that can really sidetrack business owners and cause you to make bad decisions. Here at Sarah Jones CPA, we believe that education is so powerful in helping you get rid of fear, take control of your financial health, get you where you want to go, achieve your goals, and have a full-service, all-in-one solution for you. We can do your taxes, your tax planning, your bookkeeping, your payroll, CFO services, estate planning, and walk beside you in all facets of life from beginning to end with a custom-based roadmap for success. We do it all so you can achieve your short-term goals now and your long-term goals in the future with a secure partnership with a CPA for your entire life. If that sounds like what you're looking for, you can absolutely reach out to Sarah Jones CPA.

If you want to find out more about our team and actually see our pictures and everything about us, go to sarahjonescpa.com.

You can book directly on my calendar at www.calendly.com/sarahcpa or give us a call.

If you have questions or just want more details, follow us on social media. We are everywhere. We are really big about educating and giving value there, so follow us and I would love to hear your feedback. If you have feedback on the book or anything that you'd want me to potentially add into a future edition, please reach out to me directly at sarah@sarahjonescpa.com.

Checklist 1–YOU

☐ Look at YOU.

☐ What are your values you hold to dearly? How do these integrate/operate your life and business?

☐ What is your communication style? Do you prefer frequent communication? Efficiency over details or vice versa? How do you prefer to communicate (emails, text, phone call, etc.)?

☐ Are you accountable? Are you willing to be accountable for your actions, your financial success, and will you be coachable in allowing a CPA to guide you to success?

☐ How much does fear play into your financial life? Are you willing to acknowledge this and share it with your CPA and learn to conquer it?

☐ What are your short-term and long-term financial goals? Both personal and business?

☐ What is your ideal CPA relationship? Explain what that looks like in clear detail so you can share with your potential CPA.

Checklist 2–Communication Summary

☐ Bookkeeping: reports once a month, monthly meeting to discuss operations (this can vary based on your custom engagement letter with service level)

☐ CFO/Coaching: custom dashboard with KPI and action items once a month, monthly accountability meeting with CFO and team

☐ Tax: quarterly check-ins to discuss current operations, taxable income, and proactive throughout the year

☐ Investment Services/Wealth Management: quarterly reports, bi-annual meeting with a tax/planning meeting near year end

Checklist 3–Evaluation and Interview

☐ Tell me a little about your firm, your team, and your values/ mission.

_____

_____

_____

_____

_____

☐ Are you a licensed CPA?

_____

_____

_____

_____

☐ Do you offer tax planning services?

_____

_____

_____

_____

_____

❑ What are you passionate about?

_____

_____

_____

_____

_____

_____

❑ How does your firm operate as far as operations? If I am a client, what can I expect?

_____

_____

_____

_____

_____

_____

❑ How do you handle communication?

_____

_____

_____

_____

_____

_____

❑ Do you offer newsletters, tax tips, social media insights, planning sessions, seminars? How do you communicate with your clients through the year?

_____

_____

_____

_____

_____

❑ Are you taking on new clients? How do you handle growth in your firm and making sure all clients are handled?

_____

_____

_____

_____

_____

❑ Tell me about you and your goals.

_____

_____

_____

_____

_____

_____

❑ How often do you prefer to communicate with your clients?

_____

_____

_____

_____

_____

_____

❑ What is your fee schedule like?

_____

_____

_____

_____

_____

_____

Engagement of Services Letter

Dear _____,

Thank you for taking the time to meet with me recently regarding CPA services. I understand that a CPA is a trusted advisor and a long-term partnership, and I want to make sure we are both aligned for a mutually successful relationship.

I would like to understand what it would look like for us if we chose to move forward. Can you give me some insight as to: Your office operations/procedures in place for clients?

Your office communication workflows-what should I expect as far as communication?

Your average fees for (X) services that we discussed?

How to get started with your firm?

Respectfully,

_____

Fire My CPA—Disengagement Letter

Dear _____,

Thank you for providing service to us in the past. We have decided to go a different direction and have gone through the process of selecting a CPA whom we feel is better aligned with our team and will be a long-term strategic partner. As of (Date), we will no longer need your services.

We give you permission to communicate with our new CPA if there are any questions in the transition. We appreciate you and wish you the best.

Respectfully,

_____